A12703 342342

Distinguished Studies in AMERICAN LEGAL AND CONSTITUTIONAL HISTORY

Edited by
Harold Hyman
William P. Hobby
Professor of History
Rice University

A Garland Series

Distinguished Studies in American Legal and Constitutional History

1. Gary J. Aichele. *Legal Realism and Twentieth-Century American Jurisprudence: The Changing Consensus.*

2. Kenneth R. Bowling. *Politics in the First Congress, 1789–1791.*

3. Steven R. Boyd. *The Constitution in State Politics: From the Calling of the Constitutional Convention to the Calling of the First Federal Elections.*

4. Martin J. Costello. *Hating the Sin, Loving the Sinner: The Minneapolis Childrens' Theatre Company Adolescent Sexual Abuse Prosecutions.*

5. Richard S. Eckert. *The Gentlemen of the Profession: The Emergence of Lawyers in Massachusetts, 1630–1810.*

6. C. Ashley Ellefson. *The County Courts and the Provincial Court in Maryland, 1733–1763.*

7. James C. Foster. *The Ideology of Apolitical Politics: Elite Lawyers' Response to the Legitimation Crisis of Liberal-Capitalism, 1870–1920.*

8. Patrick M. Garry. *The American Vision of the Free Press: An Historical and Constitutional Revisionist View of the Press as a Marketplace of Ideas.*

9. Robert M. Goldman. *'A Free Ballot and a Fair Count': The Department of Justice and the Enforcement of Voting Rights in the South, 1877–1893.*

10. James W. Gordon. *Lawyers in Politics: Mid-Nineteenth Century Kentucky as a Case Study.*

11. Frederick K. Grittner. *White Slavery: Myth, Ideology, and American Law.*

12. Walter T. Hitchcock. *Timothy Walker: Antebellum Lawyer.*

13. Wythe Holt. *Virginia's Constitutional Convention of 1901–1902.*

14. John W. Johnson. *The Dimensions of Non-Legal Evidence in the American Judicial Process: The Supreme Court's Use of Extra-Legal Materials in the Twentieth Century.*

15. John M. Lindley. *'A Soldier is Also A Citizen': The Controversy over Military Justice in the U. S. Army, 1917–1920.*

16. Lester G. Lindley. *The Impact of the Telegraph on Contract Law.*

17. W. Ray Luce. *Cohens v. Virginia (1821), The Supreme Court and State Rights: A Reevaluation of Influences and Impacts.*

18. Stephen Middleton. *Ohio and the Antislavery Activities of Attorney Salmon Portland Chase, 1830–1849.*

19. Stephen M. Millett. *The Constitutionality of Executive Agreements: An Analysis of United States v. Belmont.*

20. Samuel N. Pincus. *The Virginia Supreme Court, Blacks, and the Law, 1870–1902.*

21. H. D. Rosenthal. *Their Day in Court: A History of the Indian Claims Commission.*

22. Peter E. Russell. *His Majesty's Judges: Provincial Society and the Supreme Court in Massachusetts, 1692–1774.*

23. Keith R. Schlesinger. *The Power that Governs: The Evolution of Judicial Activism in a Midwestern State, 1840–1890.*

24. Stephen K. Shaw. *The Ninth Amendment: Preservation of the Constitutional Mind.*

25. John M. Spivack. *Race, Civil Rights, and the United States Court of Appeals for the Fifth Judicial Circuit.*

26. Beverly Zweiben. *How Blackstone Lost the Colonies: English Law, Colonial Lawyers, and the American Revolution.*

THE AMERICAN VISION OF A FREE PRESS

An Historical and Constitutional Revisionist View of the Press as a Marketplace of Ideas

Patrick M. Garry

Garland Publishing, Inc.
New York & London
1990

Copyright © 1990 by Patrick M. Garry.
All rights reserved.

Library of Congress Cataloging-in-Publication Data

Garry, Patrick M.
    The American vision of a free press : an historical and constitutional revisionist view of the press as a marketplace of ideas / Patrick M. Garry.
    p. cm. — (Distinguished studies in American legal and constitutional history)
    Includes bibliographical references.
    ISBN 0-8240-0022-6
    1. Freedom of the press—United States—History. 2. Press and politics—United States—History. I. Title. II. Series.
KF4774.G37   1990
342.73'0853—dc20
[347.302853]   90-36933

TABLE OF CONTENTS

Page

CHAPTER I	INTRODUCTION	1
CHAPTER II	AN HISTORICAL OVERVIEW OF THE COLONIAL AND REVOLUTIONARY PRESS	14

    A.   The Historical Literature on the Free Press Clause: A Conclusion of Uncertainty as to the Intent of the Drafters of the Press Clause 14

    B.   Printers in Colonial America: "Bulletin Boards" for their Communities 19

        1.   The Press and Business Role of an Individual Printer 19

        2.   The Colonial Press' Practice of "Impartiality" and Its Elevation to a Principle 24

    C.   The Competitive Colonial Printing Industry 29

    D.   Early Restrictions on Freedom of the Press 34

    E.   The Stamp Act and Its Influence on the American Press 41

    F.   The Political Role of the Press in Revolutionary America 46

    G.   Levy's Thesis on the Origins of the Free Press Clause 54

CHAPTER III   THE CONTEMPORARY NEWSPAPER INDUSTRY 59

    A.   The Concentration of Media Ownership . . 59

    B.   Criticisms and Concerns Over Media Concentration 61

Page

| CHAPTER IV | THE DIFFERENCES BETWEEN THE FREE SPEECH CLAUSE AND THE FREE PRESS CLAUSE . . . . 69 |

A. Introduction 69

B. The Values of a Free Press Under the Revised Marketplace Model 72

    1. The Attainment of Truth From a Competition of Diverse Ideas 72

    2. The Promotion of Representative Self-Government 74

    3. The Promotion of Society and Culture Compatible with Democratic Government 79

    4. The Value of the Press in Acting as A Watchdog on Government 86

C. The Separate Values Protected by the Speech and Press Clauses of the First Amendment 88

    1. Introduction 88

    2. The Separation of Individualistic and Societal Values in the First Amendment 89

    3. The Free Press Clause as a Positive Liberty 93

    4. The Analogy of the Press Clause to the Establishment of Religion Clause 98

D. The Free Press Guaranty: A Structural Provision of the Constitution 99

E. The Historical Basis for Interpreting the Press Clause as a Structural Provision of the Constitution 103

			Page
CHAPTER V		THE APPLICATION OF THE REVISED MARKETPLACE MODEL TO THE FUNCTIONS OF THE PRESS	108
	A.	Introduction	108
	B.	The Functions of an Individual Newspaper Protected as Negative Liberties	109
	C.	The Industry Structure of the Press Necessary to Uphold the Values of a Free Press	117
		1. A Competitive Marketplace Allowing Public Participation and the Dissemination of Diverse Opinions	117
		2. A Criticism of the Fourth Estate Model of the Press	126
CHAPTER VI		CONCLUSION	134
ENDNOTES		. . . .	141

vii

PREFACE

The revised marketplace model set forth in this book attempts to formulate a theory of the First Amendment press clause consistent with three primary concerns: the basic features of the press which the framers intended to preserve; the contemporary criticisms against media monopolization and concentration; and the essential values and functions of a free press in a democratic society. The model evolved from a social and historical focus on the press, rather than from a strictly legal focus. It borrows its name from the traditional Holmesian "marketplace of ideas" metaphor, though departing from that traditional model in its view of the role of the press and the nature of the constitutional protections of the press. More significantly, the revised marketplace model offers a clear alternative to the currently popular "fourth estate" theory of the press--a theory adopting a narrow view of the value and role of the press and contributing to the contemporary crisis surrounding the monopolized media industry. Furthermore, the historical foundations of the American press contradict many of the tenets of the fourth estate theory.

The historical inquiry underlying the revised marketplace theory explores the framer's intent not through simply their words and writings, but through the actual workings of the early American press. Such an historical inquiry had not often been used. However, recent studies of the historical background of the First Amendment have also taken a broader operational view of the early press. For instance, in <u>Printers and Press Freedom: The Ideology of Early American Journalism</u>, Jeffrey Smith sets out to examine what the framers really meant by the free press clause.[1] In doing so, Smith recognizes the value of political and cultural context in revealing the eighteenth century ideas about freedom of the press and even about the original intent of the First Amendment. Although Smith states that the meaning of press freedom in the eighteenth century consisted of many strands, he concludes that the practical experience of eighteenth century journalists pointed the nation toward a free press and produced the press clause of the First Amendment. In reconstructing several dimensions of eighteenth century free press ideology, Smith argues that defenders of a free press increasingly relied upon the image of a marketplace of ideas and the belief that competing voices produced superior conclusions. However, Smith, as does Levy, gets bogged down in analyzing the eighteenth century views on seditious libel as the baseline for free press views. Under the revised marketplace theory, this continual quarrel over whether the framers meant to do away with the law of seditious libel is left behind for a broader social and political view of the press clause.

The contemporary problems caused by concentrated ownership in the press industry and the resulting backlash against press freedoms provided a practical motivaction for the revised marketplace model. In the last several years, a flurry of books have documented the public's continued suspicion and distrust of the monopolized press. In fact, because of this public hostility and distrust, much First Amendment press law is currently arising from the relationship between the press and the public rather than from the relationship between the press and the government as was the case in the 1950's and 1960's. This public suspicion and distrust of the press is illustrated in Rodney Smolla's Suing the Press.[2] Smolla discusses and examines recent libel suits and labels the libel explosion a "cultural movement" and "one of America's newest growth industries." He recognizes the great sympathy of modern juries for libel plaintiffs and implies that this may be the result of the underlying public distrust of the press. Smolla also states that this public suspicion arose in the wake of Watergate and Vietnam--the period of the height of the fourth estate press. The public distrust of the press also follows, as suggested by Smolla, from the increasing concentration in the press industry. As the press has become more or a centralized corporate conglomerate, it has become the impersonal and powerful establishment with little accountability.

Other recent books have also documented the growing concentration in the media industry and the public fallout, and have revealed the dangers of the courts' continued adherence to a fourth estate protection of the press. In The Media Elite, the authors point out that the public has become increasingly aware that those in the media do not represent a cross-section of America.[3] According to The Media Elite, the press today conveys a dangerously slanted left wing bias in the presentation of the news. As its power is concentrated in New York and Washington, its slanted views not only carry great weight but actually distort the views of the majority of Americans. The concentrated media consequently becomes an enemy rather than a friend of democratic deliberation within a community; and the authors call upon the government to decrease the power of this concentrated and biased media.

In Manufacturing Consent: The Political Economy of the Mass Media, Edward Herman and Noam Chomsky likewise criticize the media for bias in the presentation of news, but disagree with The Media Elite as to the nature of that bias.[4] According to Herman and Chomsky, the monopolized American press conveys a very narrow range of viewpoints and subjects, and actually slants the news with a conservative view. The press, according to Manufacturing Consent, excludes the diverse views from the majority of people outside the government. As a remedy, Herman and Chomsky advocate breaking up the big media companies.

A scathing criticism of the media monopolization appears in Ben Bagdikian's The Media Monopoly.[5] Badikian outlines the adverse effects of chain-owned newspapers on the communities they serve and the censorship imposed on local editors by the parent corporation. The modern monopolized press, according to Bagdikian, does not respond to the interests of local audiences. He argues that the pressure to create editorial content not for the needs and interests of the audience but to enhance advertising has greatly intensified under chain ownership.

In the War Against the Press, Peter Stoler argues that large libel awards demonstrate that the ordinary citizens who make up juries feel estranged from and suspicious toward the press.[6] This unpopularity of the press and the rash of recent libel suits are also discussed in Richard Clurman's Beyond Malice: The Media's Years of Reckoning.[7] Clurman argues that libel suits would greatly decrease if the press would permit replies by persons who feel that they have been unfairly criticized or wounded. Similarly, the Iowa Libel Study found that libel plaintiffs, although as a group not especially litigious, sue because of their outrage at the actions of the press and because an unresponsive press often does not react or respond to the plaintiff's concerns or complaints. Thus, the lessons of Beyond Malice and of the Iowa Libel Study demonstrate that the modern press may need closer scrutiny and that a concentrated "fourth estate" press does not meet all the needs and demands of our democratic society.

These books and studies provide yet another example of the erosion and weaknesses of the fourth estate model of the press. A powerful press, without sufficient accountability and without adequate means for allowing public participation, is both a consequence of the fourth estate model and the cause of the public backlash against the press. The libel explosion in the courts reveal that the public and the press have somehow come to be disjointed. The press falls short of providing a communication link and channel for society; instead, it has come to be a powerful institution focusing more upon investigating other persons or institutions and less upon providing a social channel or marketplace for communication. A fourth estate press stands in danger of alienating the social and cultural values and functions outlined in the revised marketplace model. Indeed, with the concentrated conglomerate nature of the modern media--with its aloof corporate image rather than the personalized image of the press existing during the eighteenth and nineteenth centuries--social communication seems to be a one-sided affair. Perhaps this is the reason that plaintiffs are resorting to the only remedy they appear to have against the press and that juries are in turn granting that remedy.

The revised marketplace model set forth in this book rests upon the recognition of the role that an open and competitive press plays in the shaping and strengthening of a democratic society. Likewise, several recent studies have examined this social and cultural role of the press. For instance, in Inventing American Broadcasting, 1899-1922, Susan Douglas explores the effects of the media on communities and on the shaping of modern American society.[8] According to Douglas, the history of technology and of the media must be cultural history. James Baughman in Henry R. Luce and the Rise of American News Media also takes a cultural view of the media.[9]

Recent studies of the press appear to be increasingly taking a broader social view of the press. Instead of looking at the press from strictly a legal or journalistic view, they incorporate a social, cultural and political viewpoint. For instance, Suing the Press presents a cultural analysis of the press and of liable suits. Thus, rather than viewing the First Amendment solely through the traditional values of truth and individual fulfillment, recent studies have revealed other social values obtained from a free press and from the act of communicating.

This socially interactive aspect of the press is illustrated in The Tolerant Society.[10] Professor Bollinger advocates a social interaction theory of speech based upon a social behavior model, and consequently gives a social and cultural interpretation of the First Amendment. The value of protecting extremist speech, according to Bollinger, lies in its promotion of a vitally important trait or character of society--tolerance. The tolerance theory effectively looks not so much to the substance of the speech nor to the right to speak as to the act of communicating and tolerating and to the value of such toleration to society. Thus, Bollinger relies on a community-building model of the First Amendment based on the importance of tolerance to a society. He offers a vision of a better society through exercise of the First Amendment, and sees a social value of speech in its ability to shape the character of society. According to Bollinger, free speech is the cornerstone of social conduct and behavior.

Bollinger argues that there have been few serious attempts to integrate into the general free speech discourse a more complex and realistic view of modern society. It is especially interesting to note, however, that Bollinger's theory seeks to build and promote a certain type of society rather than a certain type and quality of government, as the classical model of free speech seeks to do.

Bollinger's social-based theory of free speech and his social interaction theory of the First Amendment gives potent ammunition to critics of the fourth estate model of the free press clause. The fourth estate model focuses primarily on the role of an unchecked press in acting as a powerful institutional watchdog on the excesses of a secretive government. No concern with society, and no involvement with society: it is just the press against the government. Bollinger, however, provides a new look at the role and value of social communication and of the press as a communicative tool or forum for the promotion of tolerance and the building of community. This social function is not served by the fourth estate model; and if we are to have social communication and interaction, we must have the proper forums--an open press--in which to do so.

As *The Tolerant Society* demonstrates, recent studies of the First Amendment have focused on broader functions and roles of free expression than those envisioned in the fourth estate model. While these recent views of the First Amendment still incorporate the values of truth and supervision of government, they also reflect other values and roles of a free press--values and roles which emphasize the social, political and cultural role of the press. By expanding the vision of free press, the functions and roles of the press are also expanded.

Contrary to the fourth estate model, which envisions the press primarily as informing a passive audience, there is an increasing recognition of the press as a mechanism in which to achieve greater citizen communication and political participation. In <u>The Electronic Commonwealth: The Impact of the New Media Technologies on Democratic Politics</u>, the authors analyze the new electronic media in terms of its impact and contribution to democracy.[11] The focus of the study is on the political impact of the new media. <u>The Electronic Commonwealth</u> examines closely the relationship between the new media and our democratic values and political system. It warns that used unwisely the mass media can become a disease insofar as it turns active citizens into passive spectators, and that it can eliminate collective deliberation in favor of simply soliciting immediate responses from isolated individuals. These are all dangers present in the fourth estate model of the press. A participatory press, on the other hand, is needed to keep alive the democratic structure of society. For instance, throughout the twentieth century, democratic movements in closed societies, such as in Africa and in some communist countries, have begun with first establishing a more communicative society--a web of voluntary neighborhood and civic associations that break the ruling party or government's monopoly on information and organization.

The new awareness of the social and participatory value of the press, and the increased criticism of a concentrated media, contradicts the fourth estate theory's emphasis on the press as a large, powerful investigative body. Indeed, because newspapers have become so large and corporate-oriented, they have tended to become more homogeneous, prudent and mainstream. Whereas opinion used to be the central ingredient of early newspapers, the media barons of today celebrate its absence. According to Thomas Griffith, the attitude of the conglomerate press today is that opinions do not really matter.[12] In fact, opinion in American journalism, particularly of the outspoken kind, has been relegated largely to small circulation journals of opinion. Although most newspapers today prosper in their unchallenged monopolies, they seem to have little character of their own and reflect no real viewpoint, need or region.

The revised marketplace model set forth in this book seeks to renovate the participatory value of the press by also elevating its emphasis on opinion. Journalism, under the fourth estate theory, has fucused primarily on the function of investigative reporting by trained professionals. What has been ignored is the opinion role of the press and the broader social role that the press plays in modern democratic society.

FOOTNOTES

1. Jeffrey A. Smith, *Printers and Press Freedom: The Ideology of Early American Journalism* (New York: Oxford University Press, 1988).

2. Rodney A. Smolla, *Suing the Press: Libel, the Media and Power* (Oxford: Oxford University Press, 1986).

3. S. Robert Lichter, Stanley Rothman, Linda S. Lichter, *The Media Elite: America's New Powerbrokers* (Maryland: Adler and Adler, 19860.

4. Edward S. Herman and Noam Chomsky, *Manufacturing Consent: The Political Economy of the Mass Media* (New York: Pantheon Books, 1988).

5. Ben H. Gadikian, *The Media Monopoly* (Second Edition, Beacon Press, 1987).

6. Peter Stoker, *The War Against the Press: Politics, Pressure and Intimidation in the 80's* (New York: Dodd, Mead, 1986).

7. Richard M. Clurman, *Beyond Malice: The Media's Years of Reckoning* (New Brunswidk, N.J.: Transaciton Books, 1988).

8. Susan J. Douglas, *Inventing American Broadcasting, 1899-1922* (Baltimore: Johns Hopkins University Press, 1987).

9. James L. Baughman, *Henry R. Luce and the Rise of the American New Media* (Boston: Twayne, 1987).

10. Lee C. Bollinger, *The Tolerant Society: Freedom of Speech and Extremist Speech in America* (Oxford: Claredon Press, 1986).

11. Jeffrey B. Abramson, F. Christopher Arterton and Gary R. Orren, *The Electronic Commonwealth: The Impact of the New Media Technologies on Democratic Politics* (New York: Basic Books, 1988).

12. Thomas Griffith, "Press Lords and Media Barons," *Gannett Center Journal* (Winter, 1989).

CHAPTER I

INTRODUCTION

Despite a general belief in free press, the courts have developed no comprehensive theory on freedom of the press and its protection under the First Amendment. Indeed, according to Professor Emerson, the outstanding fact about the First Amendment today is that the Supreme Court has never developed any comprehensive theory of what that constitutional guarantee means and how it should be applied in concrete cases.[1] Furthermore, the conditions in the media industry, to which the free press guarantee must be applied, have changed greatly in the past two centuries. The general competitive nature in the newspaper industry has declined greatly because of the disappearance of many daily newspapers and the increased concentration of ownership in the newspaper industry.[2]

Freedom of the press cases have come only recently to the United States Supreme Court.[3] At the same time, during the past two decades, scholars have paid an extraordinary amount of attention to developing a comprehensive First Amendment theory.[4] The diverse doctrinal patterns of the Court's decisions and the degree of disagreement among numerous scholars, however, illustrate a sharp lack of consensus about the meaning, scope, and application of the free press clause of the First Amendment.[5] For instance, different free press theories or models have been developed in response to the different types of communication.[6] One model is the "no regulation" model, which is most notably embodied in the treatment of newspapers, magazines and books. The second model is the common carrier model, used with the telephone and telegraph industries. Finally, there is the regulatory model, represented by the Federal Communications Commission (FCC) licensing and regulation of radio and television and incorporating a considerable degree of the kinds of content regulation that would be impermissible if imposed upon books or newspapers.[7]

The Supreme Court decisions handed down in the last two decades also demonstrate the Court's confusion about how the freedom of the press and freedom of speech clauses are related.[8] The first area of confusion in the Court exists over whether the free press clause provides a separate protection from the free speech clause. The Court has never affirmatively given independent significance to the press clause.[9] It has not, for instance, given the press any more protection than an individual enjoys under the speech clause.[10] According to some scholars, the Supreme Court has been unwilling to interpret the free press clause of the First Amendment as anything other than a guarantee of free speech for the press. Historical studies of the original intent behind the press clause have provided little guidance. Though the question of whether the framers intended an independent role for the press has been hotly debated, there seems no historically sound conclusion.[11]

While the Court certainly has not ignored the press clause, but no Supreme Court decision has rested squarely on the press clause independent of the speech clause. For instance, even if the cases on prior restraint, libel, and contempt are considered press clause cases, the same results would be reached today under the speech clause.[12] Yet though the Court has never explicitly given the press clause independent significance, it also has not foreclosed such a treatment.[13] In several decisions, the Court has apparently recognized that the two different clauses may embody or protect different freedoms.[14]

The second area of confusion in the Court is over the nature of freedoms protected by the free press clause, assuming that clause is determined to be different from and independent of the free speech clause. Among those scholars and judges believing in the independence of the two clauses, numerous conflicting interpretations of the free press clause exist.[15] The theory most visible and influential at the present time was first advocated on the Court by Justice Stewart and holds that the free press clause gives structural protection to the institutional press as a "fourth estate" to check and expose the abuses of government.[16] Under this view, the press provides expert scrutiny and supervision of government and serves as a fourth competitive unofficial "branch" of government alongside the three official branches of government.[17]

Of course, criticisms of this fourth estate view of the press abound. It is argued that by seeking special status and protection the press would invite additional regulation.[18] Other First Amendment theorists agree with Justice Stewart that freedom of the press is a right distinct from freedom of speech, but differ from the fourth estate theory in their belief that the press serves as the primary channel for democratic dialogue among the public.[19]

The nature and extent of the press clause protection depends upon the particular values and functions protected by a free press. It also depends upon a determination of whether the clause is individualistic or structural. The former would focus upon "press" acts of individuals--i.e., protecting individuals as they act in a press-related manner like publishing or gathering news. The latter looks at the protections given to the press as a structural part of our society. Differing opinions on this nature of the press clause have in turn led to differences over the type of specific judicial protections granted under the First Amendment.

Coinciding with a lack of consensus on the meaning of the free press clause is a great deal of public criticism and distrust of the press. This criticism and distrust is in turn reflected in the increasing political movements seeking to cut back on the power and freedom of the press. Moreover, underlying many of these attacks on the press lies a reaction against the current state of media ownership.

The media are becoming increasingly more concentrated in the hands of fewer and fewer corporations.[20] Increased media concentration has been criticized on the following grounds: (1) that it poses a danger to diversity of ideas and a frustration of the concept of a marketplace of ideas;[21] and (2) that such concentration frustrates citizen participation in government.[22]

Thus, each loss of a competing newspaper provokes much public concern. For instance, shortly after the shutdown of the St. Louis Globe-Democrat, its loss was lamented as leaving St. Louis with only one regional newspaper and as shrinking to fifty the number of U.S. cities with independently owned, editorially competitive dailies.[23]

The increasing monopolization and concentration of the media, with its adverse impact on the public's ability to access the press, demonstrates that government infringement may no longer constitute the primary threat to a free press. Consequently, in many ways the focus of efforts to protect a free press has shifted from the government to the corporate conglomerate. Consider for instance the example of the black press in America. By 1940, it had grown significantly.[24] It endured and survived government harassment during World War II, largely because government suppressive actions were restrained by various departments and individuals within the government itself. Although the black press survived government suppression, however, it could not outlast the trend of media concentration in the post-war decades. The black press gradually withered away not because of the reactionary hand of government, but because of the factors leading to a general decline of competitive, independent newspapers.

The courts have been well aware of the importance of a competitive media and of the dangers posed by the increased concentration of ownership in the media industry.[25] With this awareness, the courts have allowed the FCC to promulgate regulations on media ownership and concentration.[26] The courts have also applied antitrust doctrines to regulation of the mass media, not only as a matter of sound economic policy but as a means of achieving diversity of ownership and hence diversity of ideas.[27] Indeed, growing fears that media concentration threatens free expression and the democratic fabric of American society have led to governmental efforts to regulate media ownership through an affirmative diversification policy.[28]

The traditional law of free press has in the past rested on the assumption that presses are in sufficient abundance that, if government simply stands back, people will be able to express themselves freely.[29] It is doubtful, however, that the framers of the Constitution ever considered that economies of scale would create a monopolistic press or that media conglomerates could become society's gatekeepers of information.[30] Moreover, the recent criticism of the increased concentration in the media illustrates certain shortcomings of current First Amendment free press law. First, if these concerns are not addressed, they may bring cutbacks and abridgements of freedom of the press in other areas. Second, the criticism suggests that a judicial focus on protecting free speech may not adequately protect a free press. And third, it also indicates that the courts may have to reassess the values served by a free press, the differences between the values of free speech and of free press, and the protections granted by the press clause itself. Indeed, a theory of the press clause must address the major criticisms, problems and inadequacies of the contemporary press.

This book responds to such criticism and to the need for a comprehensive theory of the press clause. It argues that the speech and press clauses differ in the scope and nature of their protections. Whereas the speech clause is individualistic in nature and inures primarily to speech activities, the press clause is structural and attaches more to the press industry. This structural nature, however, is not in the form of creating and protecting a "fourth estate" press. Rather, the structural nature of the press clause lies in protecting an open and competitive press. The revised marketplace model, as proposed here, expresses and incorporates this view of the press clause.

The "revised marketplace" model--based somewhat on a literal or physical interpretation of the long-standing "marketplace of ideas" metaphor--looks more to the structure and makeup of the press industry, and less to its particular powers, than does the "fourth estate" model proposed by Mr. Justice Stewart. This revised marketplace model, however, must also be distinguished from the traditional Holmsian "marketplace of ideas" metaphor.

A traditional model of the free press clause, and one which has recently lost favor because of the monopolistic media industry, has been that of the marketplace of ideas.[31] Professor Barron tried to resurrect this model when he called for a right of access to newspapers:[32]

> Our constitutional theory is in the grip of a romantic conception of free expression, a belief that the "marketplace of ideas" is freely accessible. But if there were ever a self-operating marketplace of ideas, it has long since ceased to exist.[33]

Rather than invigorate the "marketplace of ideas" model, however, Barron tried to remedy its disappearance by calling for a right of access to newspapers. As with other critics, Barron accepted the death of the marketplace metaphor because of the degree of monopolistic concentration of the media.

The marketplace of ideas rationale was first used as a value and justification of free speech. In the early twentieth century, Holmes and Brandeis sought to protect speech largely on pragmatic grounds of social value. The marketplace of ideas rationale resulted and throughout the twentieth century formed a powerful image in the rhetoric of freedom of expression.[34] According to the marketplace model, individual speech was protected because it brought diversity, competition and efficiency to the collective search for truth. Free speech led to an expression of many ideas and, therefore, to a resulting marketplace of ideas. However, the marketplace metaphor espoused by Justice Holmes, resting upon the attainment of truth from a marketplace of ideas, served as a justification for the protection of speech and the press rather than as a true model of the press.[35] Yet, because of the increased concentration of ownership in the media industry, critics attacked this traditional marketplace model since a true marketplace in the press has ceased to exist.

Modern critics of the marketplace model have articulated several concerns with the continued validity of such a model. For instance, since the model seemingly focuses exclusively on the value of efficiency, critics argue that it could shortchange the value of individual integrity and instead simply maximize the amount of speech in the system.[36] Furthermore, Justice Stewart argues that the marketplace model gives insufficient weight to the institutional autonomy of the press.[37]

Despite these various concerns, a major reason for criticism of the traditional marketplace model is that competition and open access no longer exist in the newspaper industry. An assumption behind the First Amendment, and the marketplace model, was that any writer could gain access to a printing press without the help of government.[38] Consequently, when the emerging broadcast media threatened to create natural monopolies, the government quickly imposed regulations ensuring access and diversity of ownership and content. Such regulations illustrate society's deep concern with concentrated ownership in the media and society's desire for a diverse source of ideas and for a broad-based citizen participation in social communications. This desire is frustrated by the current state of the newspaper industry and by the realization that it no longer performs a marketplace function.

Because of the concentrated ownership of the media, the degree of citizen participation in and access to the social communication system has declined. Therefore, jurists and scholars are turning to other models to analyze First Amendment law. However, just because the nature of the press industry today is not conducive to producing diverse speech reflecting a marketplace of ideas, it is not necessary to altogether abandon the marketplace metaphor on the assumption that our First Amendment theory should be based upon a recognition and approval of the current conditions and trends in the newspaper industry.

Both advocates and critics of the traditional marketplace model focus on the total amount of speech communicated. Since the marketplace model has been closely tied with the "search for truth" value of the First Amendment, its success and legitimacy rises simply with the increase in ideas being communicated. However, the revised marketplace theory, unlike the old marketplace metaphor, does not only consider the total amount of diverse speech present in the system. The revised marketplace model focuses as much to the source and dynamics of the ideas as it does to the diversity and content of ideas. Whereas the goal of the Holmesian marketplace model was primarily the attainment of truth, the goals of the revised marketplace model are several--truth, individual and social interaction, citizen participation in public affairs, the improvement of self-government and the creation of an institutional forum to serve as a channel of communication for society.

While the traditional marketplace of ideas concept has been used to justify the protection of free speech, the revised marketplace model holds that the provision and assurance of a marketplace of open, independent and competitive presses lies at the core of the First Amendment free press clause. Under this model, the free speech clause protects the content of expression, and the free press clause provides a forum for that expression and a means by which citizens can participate in the political process and form political majorities. The structural dimension of the free press clause, under the revised marketplace model, is one of an actual marketplace of communication forums. The revised marketplace model entails a literal interpretation of the free press clause--namely, freedom of "the press." Thus, the press clause does not merely extend protection to the speech rights of an individual who prints his or her opinions, but accords protection to "the press" and the maintenance of an independent, competitive press in society. This interpretation draws a clear line between speech rights and press rights.

In formulating a distinction between the free press guarantee and the free speech guarantee, the revised marketplace theory set forth in this book outlines the distinct values and functions of a free press and creates a comprehensive theory of the press clause. This positivist approach marks a sharp departure from the negativist methodology normally employed in First Amendment adjudication. Traditionally, the Court has created First Amendment doctrines in reaction to suppressive measures instituted by the government. Therefore, press law has evolved more as a negative response to various restrictive measures than as a result of a broad and comprehensive view of a free press. Furthermore, the view of the press set forth in the revised marketplace model is formed not simply by narrowly analyzing the current legal treatment of the press but by incorporating an analysis of the social, political and economic roles of the press into a legal theory. The result of this approach is a conclusion that the press clause is structural in nature; and that this structural aspect is better described by the revised marketplace model than by the fourth estate model. This conclusion also finds support in an historical analysis of the press industry at the time of the drafting and ratification of the First Amendment. An analysis of the early American press industry shows that the revised marketplace model fits better with the framer's intentions than does the fourth estate model.

According to the current literature, there is little historical guidance on the framers' intent regarding the free press clause.[39] Furthermore, the little historical evidence that does exist leads to some radically different interpretations, i.e., from Levy (the First Amendment as strictly protecting against prior restraint) to Justice Stewart (the First Amendment as creating a fourth estate). While most historical studies on the drafting and adoption of the First Amendment have analyzed what the framers said and wrote, few have examined the conditions of the press industry that existed at the time the First Amendment was drafted and adopted. These conditions will be the focus of the historical inquiry of the revised marketplace model. Thus, the framers' intent will be determined through an examination of the role of the press during the constitutional period, with the assumption that the framers intended to preserve the kind of press with which they were familiar.

A final aspect of the revised marketplace theory is its application here only to print media. Many scholars have addressed the "double standard" that exists in First Amendment law toward print and broadcast media. Indeed, many scholars argue that the difference in standards between print and broadcast media is unjustified.[40] They contend that the two types of media should function under the same First Amendment standards. Though many distinctions between print and broadcast media have eroded, some may still exist. For instance, the print media historically and practically is more conducive to the dissemination of public opinion than is the broadcast media. Nonetheless, the values and functions of a free press, and the resulting theory of the free press clause, articulated in the revised marketplace model could be applied to all forms of media. Therefore, for the sake of simplicity and because a historical analysis of the eighteenth century press involves only print media, the revised marketplace theory presented here will discuss only First Amendment law as applied to and relating to the print media.

CHAPTER II

AN HISTORICAL OVERVIEW OF THE COLONIAL AND
REVOLUTIONARY PRESS

A. The Historical Literature on the Free Press Clause: A Conclusion of Uncertainty as to the Intent of the Drafters of the Press Clause

The value of a free press became apparent in many important ways to Americans during the revolutionary and constitutional periods.[41] The early political campaigns for resistance to British laws and then for independence were transformed into effective national movements by the press. A free press was useful not only in arousing popular support for the revolutionary cause but also in shaping new national political institutions. Following the war, the press played a key role in the determination of the kind of national government to be formed.[42]

Although the American press assumed a larger and more dynamic role in expressing and shaping opinion during the revolutionary period, this role was essentially the result of an uncharted pragmatic process that did not lead to the formation of a clear concept of freedom of expression at the time.[43] Despite the active press and its value in political protest and constitution-making, Americans during the eighteenth century did not arrive at a sophisticated definition of freedom of the press. American editors of the time were indeed committed to something called freedom of the press; but these editors and political leaders never arrived at the unequivocal position presently accepted that newspapers should be immune from penalties for their criticism of government.[44] Colonial printers certainly did not view government as open to the same scrutiny by the press as it is today.[45]

The eighteenth-century defenders of a free press were also inconsistent about who should enjoy the freedom and the degree of freedom that existed.[46] The history of the colonial period reveals that Americans were far from hospitable to unorthodox opinions.[47] For instance, as the anti-British cause gained in strength in the Colonies, patriot printers closed their papers to the Tory viewpoint and refused to honor the Tories' claim to publicly espouse their own cause through the press.[48] Thus, according to most historians, the American contribution to a libertarian theory on freedom of speech and press was strikingly absent for most of the eighteenth and early nineteenth centuries.[49] Indeed, prior to the drafting of the First Amendment, no American consensus on press freedom existed. Yet the question still exists as to what the framers intended to protect with the First Amendment.

Determining the intent of the constitutional framers nearly always arouses strong disagreement and differing interpretations among both constitutional historians and legal scholars. However, there is universal agreement on one historical conclusion regarding the press clause: the true intent of the First Amendment's authors cannot be derived from the text of the First Amendment or from the debates surrounding the drafting or ratification of the First Amendment.[50] While historians and jurists have reached various conclusions about the meaning of the press clause, there is broad agreement that the documentary history of the First Amendment itself reveals little of the framers' intent. The sparse history of the drafting of the Bill of Rights is inconclusive regarding the intent underlying the specific wording of the First Amendment.[51] And the legislative history of the press clause itself leads only to speculative and inconclusive judgments.[52] Many scholars have even concluded that no historical evidence supports a finding that the framers intended an independent role for the press apart from that protected by the speech clause.[53]

In *Legacy of Suppression*, Leonard Levy argues that the colonists gave little independent thought and even less expression to a theory of a free press. Levy notes that the debate on the Bill of Rights during ratification was conducted with vague rhetorical references to freedom of press, but without precise definition as to the meaning of that freedom.[54] Neither the great Bill of Rights advocates nor the newspapers nor the ratifying conventions provides insight.[55] Levy theorizes that much of the whole Bill of Rights controversy and the wording of the First Amendment as finally enacted arose from the political struggle between those favoring strong state and those favoring strong central government.[56]

The existing historical evidence therefore leads to several conclusions about the framers' intentions, but cannot justify any one set of conclusions.[57] Several scholars, for instance, believe that the framers only intended to eliminate prior restraint.[58] And wide disagreement exists among historians over whether the framers intended the First Amendment to prohibit prosecutions for seditious libel. Certainly no evidence exists that the framers thought in terms similar to those which are so familiar and widely accepted today.[59] It is not even certain that the framers themselves knew what they had in mind.[60] Most probably, few clearly understood what they meant by the free press clause.[61] It is even doubtful that those few agreed except in a generalized way, and it is equally doubtful that they represented a consensus.[62]

The Supreme Court recently came to the same conclusion of uncertainty that Levy and others have reached. Writing for the majority in <u>Minneapolis Star & Tribune v. Minnesota Commissioner of Revenue</u>, Justice O'Connor stated:

> In general, though, we only have limited evidence of exactly how the Framers intended the First Amendment to apply. There are no recorded debates in the Senate or in the States, and the discussion in the House of Representatives was couched in general terms, perhaps in response to Madison's suggestion that the representatives not stray from simple acknowledged principles.[63]

Given the multitude of studies done to determine the intent of the framers of the press clause and the near unanimous conclusion that such studies can only produce uncertain conclusions, nothing further can be gained from investigating the framers' intent through their words and writings. Yet we need not give up completely on all efforts to discover intent. A precise statement of intent may be impossible to find, but a picture of it may be available. Perhaps historical inquiries have focused on the wrong subject. Perhaps the historical focus should be on the nature and structure of the actual press industry existing at the time of the adoption of the First Amendment. Such an examination may provide insight into the meaning and purpose of the words used in the press clause. The assumption is that the framers would have wanted to protect the type of press structure and industry existing at the time they drafted the First Amendment. This type of historical approach was suggested by the Commission on the Freedom of the Press when it speculated on the meaning of freedom of the press at the time of the Constitution by focusing on the actual workings of the colonial press.[64] Levy likewise argues that:

> "When the framers of the First Amendment provided that Congress shall not abridge the freedom of the press they could only have meant to protect the press with which they were familiar and as it operated at the time. They constitutionally guaranteed the practice of freedom of the press. They did not adopt its legal definition as found in Blackstone or in the views of libertarian theorists.[65]

Levy also states that the free press clause recognized and strove to perpetuate the existing conditions in the late eighteenth century press industry.

Currently, many jurists reject any attempt to discover the intent of the framers. They argue that "original intent" is impossible to determine.[66] This argument, however, presumes that the intent sought is a narrow, fixed statement articulated more than two hundred years ago. To the contrary, an historical examination of the workings and conditions of the press during the constitutional period will provide a broader, more fluid definition of intent that can be applied to modern applications of the press clause.

B. **Printers in Colonial America: "Bulletin Boards" for their Communities.**

1. <u>The Press and Business Role of an Individual Printer</u>

During the colonial period, printers ordinarily edited and published their own newspapers.[67] The typical colonial newspaper consisted of four compactly printed pages, roughly ten by fifteen inches in size and somewhat smaller than a modern tabloid.[68] The papers were often difficult to read because of the smallness of the print.

The printer-editors, however, did not write most of the articles and essays appearing in their newspapers. They or their journeymen in fact wrote only a few local items. For the majority of the contents of their newspapers they solicited contributing pieces from outside authors and subscribers. These contributors commonly supplied essays on social topics or public affairs. The essays covered subjects all the way from politics to morals and religion.[69] Despite the reliance on outside contributors, the printer/editor still occupied the central role in actually publishing and distributing the newspaper. The printer also supervised the circulation and secured the advertising that could spell the difference between success and failure.[70]

Compared with the larger printing operations in England, even the most successful printing shops in the American colonies were modest enterprises.[71] Newspapering in the colonial period was not a secure business.[72] The threat of competition and of an exodus of subscribers continually prevailed. Colonial printers consequently were forced to diversify, to broaden their publishing activities, and thus to play more varied roles in their communities than was customary for English printers.[73] To supplement their incomes, for instance, publishers printed advertisements and public announcements for which they would be paid by the government.[74] Whenever they could, publishers also doubled as postmasters.[75] Interestingly, the position of postmaster carried an advantage beyond the financial compensation given to a postmaster. Benjamin Franklin, while acting in that capacity in Philadelphia in 1740, temporarily barred a competitor from the mail, alleging as his reason the competitor's tardiness in paying his postal bill.[76]

The role of the public printer was especially important in the southern colonies.[77] Close ties between government and the press existed in most of the southern colonies.[78] The governor of the colony appointed and paid the public printer. Many of the southern weeklies in fact remained adjuncts of the colonial government, and most received government support in one way or another.[79]

Because of the public support and government subsidies, only one newspaper usually existed in each colony. This pattern continued up until the late 1760s. Indeed, most of the newspapers could not have survived without subsidies.[80] These public subsidies, however, imposed an informal censorship on the printers. For instance, whether a printer published opinions against the Stamp Act often determined whether a printer would remain as the public printer.[81] Only after more newspapers started up in the revolutionary period did this type of censorship end.

Government printing along with a combination of publishing activities, i.e. newspaper publishing and job printing, therefore provided the key to economic success for colonial printers. This broad range of activities also unavoidably involved a colonial printer in a broad range of local affairs.[82] Yet, however lofty their aspirations or diversified their business, colonial printers were by training and community attitudes simple mechanics.[83] Until 1765, most newspapers, handbills, and pamphlets were produced by printers who had learned their trade as apprentices and who had earned enough to buy their own press equipment.[84] The economics of the printing business, however, did not permit most printers to become wealthy or prominent members of their communities. Furthermore, according to the conventional social prejudices at the time, the colonial printer was not commonly expected to possess a "mind of his own"; and this expectation was likely to undercut whatever efforts he made to influence his neighbors.[85]

Another weakness in the position of the colonial printer, needing all the business he could get, was that he had to take pains to please all customers at all times.[86] Hence, the colonial printer attempted to serve all of the diverse interests in his community. In short, in their quest for solvency, printers strove to be all things to all persons.[87] Consequently, colonial newspapers usually contained what their subscribers wanted said. These efforts generally paid off, and as the colonial period advanced printers experienced an increase in their circulations.[88]

The content of colonial newspapers closely mirrored the attitudes and desires of the community. Political discussion in the press was geared to the issues important to the local constituencies. Newspapers contained everything from advertisements to literary essays, political polemics, and news.[89] Essentially, colonial newspapers were bulletin boards for their communities.[90] They were both subject to and responsive to the wishes of colonial society.

An important use of newspapers by community leaders of the period was the publication of debates in the form of letters to the editor.[91] Community leaders relied on the press to express public debate through publication of these letters. In general, newspapers and political pamphlets contained basically the same material. Political essays and contributions from subscribers constituted a large proportion of the contents of a newspaper.[92] Only a rare newspaperman found the time or possessed the ability to write essays of his own.

The pivotal role in gathering information and opinions was held not by the printer but by his contributors and information sources. Although most printers published and edited their own newspapers, the contributors to colonial newspapers were generally people other than the printer.[93] Editors and printers relied on professionals who would supply the editor or printer on a fairly frequent basis with contributions on social topics or public affairs. According to Emery, the majority of editors envisioned their jobs as providing opportunities to express partisan views on social topics and public affairs.[94] In this sense, the press served as an organ through which the literate elite could, and very often did, voice their political and social opinions.[95]

Newspapers provided opportunities to the elite to express themselves and to influence public opinion.[96] Yet the elites, while desiring to voice their opinions, were often hesitant to reveal their identities. For this reason, the use of pseudonyms was a common method by which individuals published their views and at the same time attempted to conceal their identities.[97]

Printers also used pseudonyms in an attempt to protect themselves from both mob reprisals (in the event that they had printed something unpopular) and charges of libel.[98] Printers could then claim that they did not know, because of the pseudonym, the identity of the true author. In this way, printers implied that they reserved the right to print everything and anything submitted to them and that an individual had the right to have his or her opinions published.

Though printers occupied precarious financial and social positions, and though most colonial Americans could not afford newspapers, the colonial newspapers carried an inordinate level of influence. Although out of the financial reach of many individuals, newspapers were almost certainly available in many taverns. Outside of the relatively few towns, physical access to the newspapers also presented a formidable problem to all but those wealthy enough to subscribe. Nevertheless, multiple readership was still quite common in rural areas, and newspapers frequently circulated beyond the original recipient.[99]

Physical access alone, however, did not determine influence. It is not true that the press failed to influence individuals who neither received nor read the newspapers. The wide geographic distribution of newspapers among militia officers, ministers, and other leading persons led to the verbal dissemination of newspaper content.[100] In the premodern colonial society, prominent persons were expected to be teachers and leaders, and they could not have fulfilled those roles without the aid of newspapers.[101]

2. The Colonial Press' Practice of "Impartiality" and Its Elevation to a Principle

To please most of the customers most of the time, colonial printers followed a practice of impartiality. Printers often justified this trade strategy in elevated terms, professing devotion to liberty of the press and stating that a press was free only if it was open to all parties.[102] Merrill Jensen has written that "most publishers believed it was a part of their duty to print materials on all sides of a question even when they were counter to a particular publisher's own views."[103] Whatever may have been the social utility of granting access to all viewpoints, printers were attracted to the principle of impartiality because it suited their business interests to serve all customers.

One of the best known colonial arguments for an impartial press was Franklin's "Apology for Printers." According to Franklin, "printers are educated in the belief that when men differ in opinion, both sides ought equally to have the advantage of being heard by the public."[104] This principle coincided with eighteenth-century doctrines of the public good defined in terms of free competition among individuals. This was a very "mechanical" point of view.

Franklin's "Apology" offered on behalf of printers a formulation of principles usefully consistent with the trade strategies required by an underdeveloped economy.[105] The chief difficulty, as Franklin and other printers well knew, was to persuade their subscribers to recognize the legitimacy of this strategy. Such a policy of neutrality, though acceptable enough in normal circumstances, was often impossible to follow in times of bitter controversy. Since "the business of printing has chiefly to do with men's opinions," as Franklin noted, printers had to live with "the peculiar unhappiness of being scarcely able to do anything in their way of getting a living, which shall not probably give offense to some."[106]

Many colonists held a printer responsible for the sentiments he published and seemed to have been unprepared to tolerate him if, caught in the middle of intense conflict, he wished to publish both sides. Thus, when attitudes polarized, a printer sometimes had to work for a single faction; otherwise he might antagonize everyone. In quieter times, printers might hope to maintain the "liberty" of their presses to print different opinions. However, to pursue it rigorously could subject a printer to severe and contrary pressure when the political scene became agitated.[107]

With the escalation of the conflict with England, printers in the colonies eventually gave up neutrality to choose sides. More than twice as many opted for the patriot side as for the Tory side.[108] Though reluctant to advertise themselves as full-fledged partisans, many printers still tried to take the middle of the road, steering to one side only when obliged.[109] Strict political neutrality, however, which had never been easy to achieve in a time of conflict, became nearly unachievable during a revolution.[110] Furthermore, during the prolonged crisis of the revolutionary period, printers also began to act in ways that promoted a politics expressive of conflict and dissent. This practice contrasted with that of the earlier colonial period when impartiality was followed more closely and when the colonial newspapers, despite being partisan, served primarily as indiscriminant forums for public debate.[111]

Most Tory printers waited as long as possible before abandoning fully the traditional principle of neutrality.[112] In fact, what often stamped particular printers as Tory sympathizers was not so much their publicly-stated political sentiments as their apparent determination to maintain neutrality. The Tory printers often made the excuse that they were simply acting in accordance with their notion of the liberty of the press.[113] However, traditional trade strategies and principles had proven ineffective in revolutionary conditions and were incapable of sustaining those American printers who had tried to keep their presses open to unpopular Tory points of view.[114]

Whether or not their motives were any more mercenary than those of their patriot counterparts, Tory printers failed to devise a rationale for their business strategies that drew effectively on the prevailing popular creed of liberty.[115] Indeed, public expectations of the role of American printers were being reshaped by the revolutionary conflict. Through the journalistic marketplace, the colonists were registering their embrace of patriot views and rejection of the Tory position. Compared with their Tory counterparts, many patriot printers reacted to the heightened political mood of the public and expressed strong political views and statements of high constitutional principle.[116] Thus, the political and opinionated journalism of the revolutionary period was market-driven, and the printers were responding either voluntarily or because of subscription pressures to the views and demands of the community they served.

Although both sides from time to time invoked the principle of freedom of the press, in reality the issue had now emerged in a new form. As far as the patriot editors were concerned, they no longer had to fear attempts at legal repression. Their greatest fear was the loss of disgruntled subscribers. In the interests of consistency, however, they felt obliged to justify their suppression of opposition writings. Thus, they contended that liberty of speech belonged solely to those who spoke the speech of liberty.[117] To British supporters, such talk was hypocrisy. Being now the underdogs, they insisted that freedom of the press required editorial impartiality.[118]

Very gradually there arose from the revolutionary experience a revised understanding of the role of an American printer. Responding to a new belief that sharply antagonistic opinions might properly be articulated in the public forum, printers in America began to discard their neutral trade rhetoric and to behave aggressively and unapologetically as partisans. Consequently, the increasingly opinionated newspapers reflected the intense ideological content of revolutionary politics.

For much of the eighteenth century, American printers had followed business and political strategies that sometimes impeded the flow of diverse and dissident opinion into the public forum.[119] During the revolutionary years, however, the trade adapted to the new politics of controversy. By so doing, printers became major figures in the political life of the republic. Long after independence, newspapers continued to express political opinion; and partisan journalism became a well-established feature of American politics.[120] As the Reverend Samuel Miller observed at the start of the nineteenth century, the newspapers of America were "immense, moral and political engines" that advanced opinions as well as reported occurrences.[121] By 1800, political opinion had become the staple of American journalism.

C. The Competitive Colonial Printing Industry

It is important to note the newspaper industry that faced the framers of the First Amendment in 1791. In the American colonial and revolutionary experience, the communications media had been comprised of many small enterprises.[122] Easy entry existed into the pamphlet, book and newspaper publishing industry. An individual wishing to communicate to the reading population could readily do so in one of several ways. First, he could go through an apprenticeship and become a master printer himself.[123] Second, he could hire a printer and furnish him with a shop, though instances of this type of entry were rare.[124] And third, an individual who desired to print his own views could induce the publisher of a newspaper with established readership to publish his essay.[125]

The character of the American press changed considerably after 1765.[126] There were thirty-seven newspapers published in the colonies at the time of the battles of Lexington and Concord.[127] By 1781 there were thirty-five newspapers; but in the interim seventeen of the original thirty-seven had ceased publication and another thirty-three had appeared, of which only fifteen survived. The decade following saw an extraordinary growth in the number of newspapers. Altogether, about sixty newspapers appeared in the mid-1780s, many of which eventually stopped publication. Nevertheless, in 1790 there were ninety-two newspapers in the

United States.[128] Also, there were competing printshops in all the larger settlements after about 1730. In all, 450 newspapers were started in the period from 1783 to 1801.[129]

Competition between presses was stiff. As the conflict with Great Britain worsened, printers needed to be especially in tune to the political wishes and opinions of their local readers.[130] Thus, printers maintained a keen awareness of who their readers were and whether they harbored loyalist or patriotic tendencies. Community pressure commonly influenced printers and shaped their publishing decisions. In several documented instances, printers lost their businesses to newcomers and went out of business because they failed to respond to the local populace.[131] This danger was especially acute in large cities like Boston and Philadelphia, where a large number of presses existed.[132] In short, presses were subordinate to the wishes of society so long as society was not completely disinterested. Yet with the proliferation of newspapers, society became more and more involved and opinionated.

Another important change in the character of the press in the period from 1783 to 1791 occurred as newspapers were more and more founded as arms of political parties. Up to this time, conducting a newspaper had been chiefly a matter of selecting without much initiative the conventional items of newspaper content and printing and distributing them.[133] Newspaper operators had been primarily mere printers and publishers. However, the ardent partisan feature of journalism in the period from 1783 to 1801 had its roots deep in the revolutionary press.[134]

As partisan activity grew in the new nation, the public came to recognize an additional reason for the existence of newspapers. Many newspapers served as the spokesmen of political parties.[135] Indeed, following the war, newspapers were increasingly started as arms of political parties and began acting as semiofficial vehicles for a political party.[136] This gave a new color to American journalism and resulted in the emergence of the newspaper editor. Prior to the 1790s, nearly all newspapers had been started as auxiliaries to printing establishments, whose proprietors printed and distributed communications from outside contributors and routine selections of domestic and foreign intelligence from other papers.[137] By the turn of the century, however, newspapers came more and more to be the voices of political parties, with editors assuming responsibility for choosing and coordinating the viewpoints of their contents.[138] Yet even though newspapers became increasingly partisan, they still served as forums for public debate.

During the colonial and postrevolutionary periods, the press had been used as a vehicle for espousing the interests of one group against those of another--colonists against Royal governors, revolutionists against Tories, and generally outsiders against insiders in government.[139] Each group vied for public opinion through the press, with the challenging side praising freedom of the press because its chances for ascendancy depended upon reaching the public with its message.[140] Indeed, almost every newspaper served as a channel for public debate[141] and became a free forum for the discussion of politics.[142] Printers also adopted a new belief that sharply antagonistic opinions could properly be aired in public forums.

It was not assumed that any one newspaper would represent all or nearly all of the conflicting viewpoints regarding public issues. Together, all of the newspapers would do so. If they did not, the person whose opinions were not represented could start another newspaper.[143]

During the period preceding adoption of the First Amendment, the press was characterized by the relatively small scale eighteenth-century printshop. Obviously, it is debatable whether the First Amendment was actually adopted with the idea of preserving the press as it then existed. However, according to Owen, the First Amendment can be regarded as having at least one implicit assumption: that competition in the marketplace of ideas will be conducive to political freedom in a democratic system.[144] Owen demonstrates that the most recent experience of the framers of the First Amendment was with a highly partisan press that offered easy access to the means of reaching an audience and whose numbers were steadily growing.[145] Tracing the economic history of the colonial publishing industry, Owen argues that the American experience with freedom of expression is consistent with unregulated competition when the press is characterized by small-scale technologies and ease of entry.

An examination of the press industry preceding the adoption of the First Amendment shows that communications dominated by significant scale economies were unknown by the framers of the First Amendment. In their experience, "economic competition was consistent with the political function of the press because of the small scale technology of printing and the rapid rate of entry in the industry in the decade preceding 1791."[146] Indeed, the availability of inexpensive printing presses, along with the political ferment of the time, fueled the growth of the "penny press" in the nineteenth century. These penny presses were often started not by industrialists but by skilled workers.[147]

We cannot know whether the framers would have acted differently if they had been faced with a media structure such as exists today; however, the evidence shows that their experience was with a highly partisan press and with one in which there was great accessibility. Indeed, perhaps no thought was given to legislating a right of access to newspapers because of the relative ease of access to the presses at that time.

If, as Owen suggests, each newspaper expressed one point of view to the virtual exclusion of all others, the diversity of opinion in the postrevolutionary press depended on the number of newspapers.[148] Characterized by many publications reflecting highly partisan viewpoints, the early American press constituted a true marketplace of ideas in which there was relatively easy access to the channels of communication.[149] Speech and publishing in 1791 emanated from relatively fragmented sources rather than from integrated, highly organized media forms.[150]

It is doubtful that any clues to the eventual transformation of fragmented and diverse media enterprises into pervasive and concentrated economic and social forces existed in the late eighteenth century. The drafters of the First Amendment had no reason to anticipate a marketplace of ideas dominated by the few in command of the mass media.[151] Today, advertisers rather than consumers or publishers have emerged as the primary subsidizers of information transmission. Furthermore, since diverse public debate and easy entry into local communication forums have been largely supplanted by centralized information outlets and limited entry into the increasingly nationalized and globalized press, the free marketplace of ideas concept appears to have applicability only to the early period of the American press.[152]

D. Early Restrictions on Freedom of the Press

The movement for press freedom in America during the revolutionary period responded not only to the campaign for independence but also to the array of press restrictions instituted in the colonies by the Crown. These restrictions followed in many ways the pattern of press restrictions in England. Centuries of press regulation and the longstanding practice of prior censorship in England impressed upon Americans the need for a free press.[153]

In England, prior restraint had played a central role throughout the history of regulation over the printing presses.

Furthermore, the expansion of the printing trade had evoked a series of commercial regulations.[154] The devices of monopoly grants and limited licensing were used to regulate the press industry.[155] Through the system of government licensing, the Crown secured for itself a share of the profitable printing business.[156] Gradually, licensing also served as a convenient tool for preventing publication of certain ideas.[157]

The peak of restrictive practices aimed at the press occurred in 1586 under Elizabeth I, when a Star Chamber decree specifically limited the number of printing establishments and required all books to be reviewed by the Archbishop of Canterbury before publication.[158] The decree was enforced through the Stationers Company -- a guild of the licensed printers. In exchange for monopolistic power, printers submitted to the authority and control of the licensor. In one form or another, this licensing system established by the Star Chamber persisted until 1641.

In 1641, Parliament abolished the Star Chamber and ended the licensing system.[159] For several years following, the press had neither an effective censor nor an effective copyright protection. The disarray in the printing trade that ensued, however, finally moved Parliament to enact a new censorship enforcement system. It established a Board of Licensors in 1643 and restored enforcement authority to the Stationers Company. Censorship shifted from royal and Episcopal control to parliamentary and Puritan control. Although the monopolies of the Stationers Company were cut back, the licensing continued.

In 1694, Parliament finally permitted the Licensing Act to expire.[160] However, the basis for refusal to renew the Act was no grandiose theory of free speech but practical considerations arising from the difficulties of administration and from the restraints of trade caused by licensing.[161] For more than a century, maintenance of a licensing system had depended on the alliance between the Stationers Company and the government. As a result, a suffocating system of licensing and blanket censorship developed. The system eventually collapsed in 1694 not so much from the urge for free expression as from economic pressures for easier entry into a profitable printing business.[162] Thus, the end of licensing resulted from dissatisfaction with monopolization of the means of expression and a demand for access to the printing industry. The death of the licensing system, however, did not also bring the end of sanctions for speech critical of the government or its leaders.

Despite the existence of limits on what safely might be said, the abolition of the licensing system enabled everyone with access to a printing press to publish their opinions. Consequently, eighteenth century England witnessed a growth of political journals and journalists.[163] The majority of printers had benefited from the expiration of the licensing system and praised the virtues of its abolition.[164] By the middle of the eighteenth century, the absence of prior censorship had advanced

36

from a simple statement of fact to a principle. This principle was subsequently stated in its familiar form by Blackstone.[165]

The American colonial press witnessed similar regulation and suppression as that experienced by the English press. In 1690, America's first newspaper was suppressed by the Massachusetts government, which declared not only that publication would be suppressed but also that no future publications could be distributed without first obtaining a license or governmental appointment.[166]

Although licensing had expired at the end of the seventeenth century in England, sporadic attempts to impose prior restraints continued in the colonies until the 1720s.[167] After that date, all threat of a licensing system appears to have vanished. In the early 1720s, James Franklin published the first paper to survive in America without official sanction.[168] Franklin's paper led the first newspaper crusade in American history. For his efforts, however, James Franklin was twice thrown into prison for refusal to identify sources.[169]

In response to the licensing system, a movement started in the general population and at the constitutional convention for the enactment of limitations on federal powers in the area of free speech and press.[170] The movement against licensing paralleled a general movement in America against state-sponsored monopolies, including state-supported churches. Many historians stress that the First Amendment resulted from the framers' familiarity with previous instances of press restraint--i.e., licensing and censorship.[171]

The direct legacy of the expiration of the Licensing Act and the concomitant absence of prior restraints was the belief that expression was not reserved for the privileged few but was the common right of all people. This belief fueled the rise of American journalism and popular discussion of politics and government.[172] Along with the expiration of the Licensing Act, additional reforms like the postal reforms allowed more newspapers to gain wider audiences.[173]

Another obstacle faced by the colonial press was the power of the postmasters to hamper the delivery of objectionable matter.[174] In response to this practice, a great outcry in the press arose against the postal system.[175] James Madison wrote that for public opinion to serve as "the real sovereign," the public required a free press and particularly a free circulation of newspapers throughout the public.[176] However, postal regulations and a proposed stamp tax threatened to impede the circulation of newspapers. Madison and Jefferson not only opposed such regulations but established a Republican journal to combat the predominantly Federalist press.[177]

The government also possessed an effective financial leash on newspaper owners who did government printing.[178] Unlike the British press, however, colonial newspapers went untaxed until the Seven Years' War.[179]

In early 1790, a different type of economic restriction on the press was threatened. The postmaster general proposed a plan to tax newspapers for the use of the mails. Newspapers vehemently opposed this tax.[180] Their circulation depended on cheap mailing rates, and many opposition papers viewed this tax as a Federalist attempt to restrict the anti-administration newspapers. Some even considered the Post Office Act of 1792 to be much worse than the British Stamp Act.[181] Both editors and subscribers protested the Act and argued that it contravened the First Amendment. These efforts, along with the toleration of prosecutions for seditious libel, demonstrate that the colonial concern with press restrictions revolved around restrictions on circulation rather than on restrictions involving content.

Even though the pragmatic growth in freedom of the press in England had many parallels in America, there were more differences than likenesses in the progress of America and England toward free expression.[182] The breakdown of effective control over the press in America resulted partly from the demand for printed matter and the increase in printers and even more to the geographic diffuseness of American society. The colonies lacked both an obvious center for the printing trade and a common legal system overseeing the presses. Therefore, people wishing to publish matter that might offend the authorities in one place could usually find a neighboring jurisdiction which took a more tolerant attitude.[183]

The discontinuance of prior restraint marked a milestone in the British/American struggle for journalistic independence, but it still did not leave an editor free to publish at will. In its place, the authorities drew a distinction to be applied after publication between the liberty and the license of the press. Under this distinction, the editor could still be prosecuted for seditious libel. Even the patriot press had never denied that the press could abuse its privileges and that such abuse could be restrained. The distinction between freedom and license found its most forceful expression in a resolution published by the Committee of Inspection in Newport, Rhode Island, endorsing a boycott of James Rivington's Gazateer.[184] Moreover, the outbreak of the war did nothing to make the patriots more tolerant of opposition. Nonetheless throughout the 1780s, the issue of restraining or sanctioning the press seldom arose.[185] Even in Massachusetts, torn by a rebellion in 1786, prosecutions for sedition were brought against armed rebels and not printers.

Given the early American crusade for freedom of the press and for an open, competitive newspaper industry, many historians and jurists have argued that the spirit of that crusade should also extend to private restrictions and monopolization as well. With the concentration that has occurred in the press industry, the question has been raised whether four centuries of press struggles to break the licensing bonds of governments could end with a new variety of restraints--where the gatekeepers of information are a handful of superconglomerates.[186]

E. The Stamp Act and Its Influence on the American Press

One of the political catalysts of the American Revolution was the effort of the British to subdue the popular press in colonial America.[187] This attempt was twofold. The first was an accelerated use of the law of seditious libel. The second was the Stamp Act, under which a prohibitive tax was placed on the paper used by the presses. This tax threatened to force the inexpensive press out of circulation and thus to suppress colonial discussion of politics.

The Stamp Act passed by Parliament in 1765 proposed a host of unprecedented and, in the American view, unconstitutional taxes.[188] On the printers the Stamp Act imposed taxes and hardships affecting nearly every branch of their trade. The passage of the Stamp Act hurt printers by threatening an increase in their costs and by jeopardizing their subscription base, since many subscribers refused to even indirectly pay a tax to the Crown.

Immediately following passage of the Act, printers generally hesitated to openly defy the law, having no strong tradition of civil defiance and being still uncertain of support from their fellow citizens.[189] From the outset, however, the bolder printers had hopes of nullifying the Stamp Act. Though as time passed, printers learned that far from standing alone they had strong allies in the community. Gradually, the newspaper pages began to chronicle the mounting opposition and to spread before the public furious denunciations of the Act.[190] Indeed, the outburst of popular resentment against the Act was so great that it led to the start-up of four new newspapers.[191] Printers took an active role in the debate and developed a close alliance with political groups such as the Sons of Liberty.[192] These political groups also founded new newspapers whenever they felt it desirable.[193]

As the Stamp Act became effective, only a minority of newspapers ceased publishing altogether. The majority became inspired by the wave of public support, and some chose to defy the law openly.[194] Indeed, throughout the colonies most printers in one manner or another opposed the Stamp Act.[195] Not only did the newspapers criticize the Act, but nearly all of them continued to publish with little or no interruption. By the time the Stamp Act was repealed, newspaper printers had a heightened sense of their role in the community. The principle of "liberty of the press" had become a battle cry against the Stamp Act.[196] The campaign against the Stamp Act also increased the opinion role of newspapers. No longer "mere transmitters of information, they had become engines of opinion."[197]

The newspapers carried forward the role they had played in the Stamp Act crisis to the protest against the Townshend Acts.[198] Even more so than the Stamp Act, the Townshend Acts sparked an intense battle of opinion that was waged in the newspapers. The war of opinion and propaganda was fought between the patriot press and the government press. This contest revealed the degree of public support behind each cause. A critical moment in the protest came when the Pennsylvania Chronicle published "Letters from a Farmer in Pennsylvania."[199] The publication of the

"Farmer's Letters" touched off a journalistic warfare over the Townshend Acts. Moreover, when the British troops arrived to be quartered in the colonies the newspapers launched a journalistic offensive and established an intercolonial undercover news network to spread intensely partisan accounts of the British troops.[200]

The government reacted to the patriot campaign in the press with a propaganda campaign of its own.[201] The colonial governments attempted to wage counterattacks in their own allied newspapers and embarked upon a campaign to convince writers to contribute to their newspapers.[202] Undeterred by these efforts at counterpropaganda, however, the patriot newspapers kept up the attack and carefully chose their targets with an eye to local resentments. The patriot newspapers waged a spirited fight against the Townshend Acts and contributed to the eventual repeal of nearly all of the duties.

During the controversy surrounding the Stamp Act and Townshend Acts, printers were greatly swayed by the opinions of their readers. The more radical the readers, the bolder the printers.[203] As in New England, editors in the cities of New York and Philadelphia pursued a course dictated by local circumstances.[204] The content of colonial newspapers closely mirrored the particular issues which were important to the local constituencies.[205] The press in effect became intertwined with local partisan battles, and newspapers often started up just as political issues rose in importance.[206] For example, the newspaper campaign against the Townshend Act reflected and expressed the popular opposition to those measures.

Though the interim period between the Townshend Acts and the Revolutionary War did not see much heated political debate in print, newspapers continued to exist and to flourish. Their greatest achievement in this period was keeping open the channels of public discussion, which would become valuable in the crucial years ahead. Indeed, in the period preceding the Revolution, several newspapers served strictly as journals of opinion and did not even bother to print hard news.[207]

The era of peace and prosperity in the early 1770s produced additional newspapers.[208] Boston was still the principal center with five newspapers, followed by Philadelphia with four in English and one in German, New York with four, and Charleston with three. All of these were nonpolitical undertakings. Events were occurring, however, which would soon cause them, like their other contemporaries, to take sides in the upcoming conflict with England.

The calm ended in 1773 when Parliament passed the Tea Act. Shortly after passage, a roar of protest emerged from the northern newspapers.[209] The most aggressive editors were those who had participated in the protests in the 1760s.[210] Again, the public mood thrust the newspapers into the midst of the protest. Throughout the journalistic debate on the Tea Act, the content of the newspapers leaned more toward opinions, essays, and propaganda than toward objective news.[211] The pro-British writers, however, were neither so impassioned nor so numerous as their adversaries.[212] They suffered further from the fact that most of the press was closed to them, hence fatally restricting the number of people they could reach.

The American press played a major role in opposing British rule and specifically the Stamp, Townshend, Sugar and Tea Acts.[213] The distinct gain in prestige made by the press in the revolutionary period began with the Stamp Act, the repeal of which was recognized as the result of a united opposition by the newspapers. Contributed essays supporting and opposing British authority came to play an important role in the newspapers of the day, and coverage of American political news expanded.[214] Circulations of newspapers also greatly increased during this period. The printer himself continued mainly as a conduit for other sources of news and opinions, but it was impossible for him to remain neutral in the struggle. By the time of the outbreak of hostilities in 1775, almost every newspaper in the colonies could be clearly identified as either patriot or Tory.

In the attacks against Britain, the colonial press engaged in both sensationalism and propaganda. There did occur in some sectors of the press a reasoned examination of some of the underlying problems and issues of imperial relations. Generally, however, the newspapers did not focus on a reasoned and rational approach, but simply and ardently espoused the patriot cause. Likewise, as the journalistic battle during the Revolutionary War took on a new flavor, switching from a debate between the Whigs and the Tories to one between three different groups of patriots (the Separationists, the Reconcilers, and the Fence-Sitters), the debate in the press was intensely opinionated and partisan.[215] Editorial tolerance did not ensure sobriety of discussion. Indeed, the reverse occurred, just as it had in the debates preceding the war.[216] The newspapers thus expressed the pulse of public opinion--they did not stand apart from the subscribing public in an objective "educational" role.

In addition to its political consequences, the newspaper offensive unleashed by the Stamp Act and Sugar Act made several permanent impacts on American journalism.[217] First, the influence of the press was enormously enhanced, instilling a newspaper-reading habit which has characterized all succeeding generations. In 1800, for instance, a magazine declared the United States to have become a nation of newspaper readers, and foreign observers noted in comparison with Europe the prevalence of newspapers in America.[218] Indeed, while the American press was developing and expanding, the communications systems in the rest of the British Empire were deteriorating. Second, the number of newspapers and the frequency of publication increased. Many newspapers began to be printed two or three times a week. Finally, the dispute with Britain also established the opinion-making function of the press.

F. <u>The Political Role of the Press in Revolutionary America</u>

The revolutionary leadership attached great importance to the freedom of the press. In 1765, John Adams observed in his "Dissertation on the Canon and Futile Law" that he knew of no "means of information more sacred than a free press."[219] Throughout the revolutionary crisis, patriots generally agreed that without a free press they could never have hoped to gain independence.[220]

By the middle of the eighteenth century, the press had become a well-recognized instrument through which to conduct the business of politics. Indeed, in 1752 the first newspaper appeared that was devoted entirely to "political expose."[221] Nash notes that by the 1740s the press had become an indispensable part of politics, being used both for campaigning purposes and as a means of pressuring those already in office to adopt a particular course of action. For example, in 1754 seventeen pamphlets appeared in Boston to protest a liquor excise bill under consideration by the Massachusetts legislature, and this outburst resulted in the legislature's rejection of the bill.[222]

By the time of the American Revolution, the press had proved itself to be an invaluable tool with which to convey political messages; and during the Revolution the press fulfilled this purpose--to inform the people of the evils of British rule and to incite them to action. As the patriots found, the press could rouse the people to action, fuel the militant spirit, sustain civilian morale, and convince the public that rebellion was both right and practicable.[223] Essentially, freedom of the press was recognized by the revolutionaries because they realized that the press was necessary to keep the colonists informed and to gather support for the revolutionary cause.[224]

As hostilities with Britain escalated, however, the problems of survival for the press also increased. The scarcity of imported newsprint, the spiraling costs of domestic paper, and the shortage of printers due to wartime demands plagued newspapers throughout the colonies.[225] Nonetheless, despite the problems, the total number of newspapers on July 4, 1776 remained exactly the same as at the beginning of the year. Even in the face of higher subscription rates, all six newspapers in Philadelphia continued to publish. And it was there that the most notable discussions of independence took place.[226]

The role of the press in the conflict with Britain was enhanced by the free movement of printers from colony to colony.[227] A significant intercolonial movement of journeymen occurred, and accompanying that movement came the start-up of more newspapers. Furthermore, printers completing their journeymanship often struck out on their own.[228] Therefore, during the Revolutionary period both the presses and printers seemed relatively mobile. Unsurprisingly then, newspapermen to an unusual degree possessed a continentwide view of affairs partly from having lived in different colonies, partly because of kinship ties with printers in other colonies, and partly from a knowledge of events elsewhere about which they learned from news sent them by fellow editors. A sophisticated network of presses and printers allowed the rapid spread of news throughout the colonies.[229] For instance, the amount of intercolonial news carried by newspapers increased more than sixfold from 1730 to 1770. Therefore, as the revolutionary period progressed, printers came to think of America as a single country rather than as a collection of thirteen separate societies.[230]

Having greater impact and wider dissemination potential than any other made of communication at the time, the press became the major organ for the distribution of opinions and information during the Revolutionary period. Furthermore, as noted by Davidson, the effects and influence of written opinions outweighed that of oral communications:

> Written propaganda both complements and supplements oral propaganda. It not only reinforces by repetition suggestions given in another form, but it reaches those untouched directly by oral appeals. The influence of a sermon or public address was more than doubled when printed in a pamphlet or newspaper. The written word, moreover, carries an authority of its own--people believe what they read.[231]

Aside from the thousands of pamphlets that were published during the years 1763-83, newspapers constituted the most effective organ of propaganda during the Revolution, largely due to the larger audiences receiving newspapers.[232]

The expanding influence of the colonial and revolutionary press was reflected in the increase in the number of newspapers: in 1763 twenty-one newspapers were being published in America; by 1775 that number had doubled to forty-two.[233] Furthermore, of those forty-two newspapers, only a few were controlled by pro--British printers. This paucity of pro-British presses resulted from the failure of the Tories to begin prior to 1774 a large-scale press campaign in defense of the British.[234]

Not only were the patriot presses advancing the cause of independence, but pro-British newspapers were disappearing both because of the tactics used by the patriots to force British newspapers out of business and because of loss of subscribers.[235] According to the newly-revised colonial concept of a free press, oppression of an opposition newspaper was justified on the grounds that a free press was supposed to be an instrument of liberty expressing the cause of freedom against oppression.[236]

The expanding American press served to unify the various colonies in the cause of the revolution. The impact of the press and the content of colonial newspapers helped to unify American leaders and to estrange them from Britain.[237] Indeed, to colonial Americans the press offered a remedy for their most chronic ailment: disunity.[238] Buel notes that colonial America understood the role that newspapers could play in uniting the colonies:

> Newspapers could play a special part in welding together a united populace by disseminating knowledge of the [British] constitution, and how their ruler's actions related to it. Without such knowledge, subjects would not know when their rights were invaded, nor have a common principle on which to act.[239]

Recognition of this role and purpose of a free press may also be found in the <u>Address to the Inhabitants of Quebec</u>. The <u>Address</u> was sent to Quebec in October 1775 by the First Continental Congress in order to garner the Canadians' support in the fight against British oppression.[240] Designed to outline the rights for which they were fighting, the Continental Congress articulated the importance of freedom of the press:

> The last right we shall mention, regards
> freedom of the press. The importance of this
> consists, besides the advancement of truth,
> science, morality, and arts in general, in its
> diffusion of liberal sentiments on the
> administration of government, its ready
> communication of thoughts between subjects,
> and its consequential promotion of union among
> them, whereby oppressive officers are shamed
> or intimidated, into more honorable and just
> modes of conducting their affairs.[241]

The leaders of the American movement for independence understood the power of unity and communication offered by the press, and diligently worked to espouse their cause to the American people through an active press. After passage of nonimportation and nonconsumption agreements, for instance, the Continental Congress decided that the press could be an important tool in enforcing those resolutions.[242] This punitive function had its precedent during the Townshend Acts, when newspapers had helped discipline the foes of nonimportation regulations and had assisted in enforcing the boycott of English commerce.[243]

The press played a vital role in the movement toward independence. In fact, the press had come a long way since 1763 when its voice was relatively small. By the outset of the War for Independence, it held an essential place in the community.[244] This vital role played by the press did not escape the notice of political leaders at the time.[245] Despite the unevenness of its influence, the press consistently reflected the life and interests of the nation. At times, it both molded public opinion and mirrored it. However, seldom has the press accomplished both functions so completely as in the years immediately following the ratification of the federal Constitution.[246] The dispute with Britain had led many Americans to examine seriously the nature of government itself, and this dialogue aired in the newspapers.[247]

In the 1790s, the development of political parties led to the development of a partisan press. Both Republicans and Federalists participated in forming party presses.[248] It was quickly recognized that the new democratic nation needed a free press as a "bulletin board" of public opinion. The Republicans valued a free press because of their belief that public opinion was more than a cyclical phenomenon registering itself every two years at the polls: it was in a continuous process of formulation and could be conveyed simultaneously through the press.[249] According to Republicans, newspapers served as the best channel for conveying advice to those in power and for releasing the pent-up emotions of those out of power.[250] Whether applauded or depreciated, in reality the press was for each party the conduit between its leaders and the public.

The opinion power of the press was well recognized at the time. Indeed, Professor Smith states that by the end of the war, public opinion had become the basis of American democratic development.[251] The impact of the press during the revolutionary period had not only instilled a newspaper-reading habit in the American public, but also firmly established the opinion-making function of the press and thereby contributed substantially to the democratization of American politics.[252] Following the war, travelers from Europe frequently commented on the multiplicity of opinion journals in the United States and on their ability to both shape public opinion and to act as an accurate barometer of public opinion.

Never in the world had there been a comparable means of communicating knowledge.[253] Newspapers were published with greater frequency and in greater variety than any other form of publication. Newspapers also constituted an important tool for the political leadership. For if, as Edmund Morgan argued, the American Revolution was an intellectual movement in which politics replaced religion as the chief concern of the colonial leadership, newspapers became the equivalent of secular Bibles.[254]

Thomas Leonard illustrates the political and public discourse role of the early American press in The Power of the Press: The Birth of American Political Reporting. According to Leonard, the early press by creating a forum for the expression of political interests motivated Americans to pay attention to their government, to welcome public discourse, and to vote. To Leonard, the achievement of democratic participation was left to the press. Leonard argues that the press provided the vernacular for the discussion of issues, made political debate legitimate, and served as the chief forum for public controversy. In essence, the development of the American press led to the rise of democratic political participation.

Leonard's discussion of the value of a free press in early America centers more on the freely competitive and participatory nature of the press than on the journalistic quality of the reporting. James Franklin's <u>Courant</u> provides one such example. Every week Franklin opened the pages of the <u>Courant</u> to dissent. His leadership encouraged a wider sweep of argument in political life, and other newspapers followed his style of airing political opinions. Yet as the colonial press increasingly acted as a forum for public debate, the political criticisms expressed in the newspapers did not stem from a systematic, well-controlled media campaign, but usually amounted to a "flailing about" at various targets. This mirrored the conglomeration of views held by the public and provided an unpredictability which made the press difficult for colonial governments to control. Furthermore, the financial precariousness of newspapers drove them into the arms of factions and parties. What emerged was a predominantly partisan press, not one which provided responsible and objective political reporting. For instance, Pennsylvania newspapers published between 1776 and 1779 contained "vast amounts of some of the bitterest, most dishonest writing in American political history."[255]

G. <u>Levy's Thesis on the Origins of the Free Press Clause</u>

Leonard Levy has, in <u>Emergence of a Free Press</u>, substantially revised and enlarged his theories put forth in 1960 in the publication of <u>Legacy of Suppression</u>, his highly influential book on freedom of expression in early American history. In <u>Legacy of Suppression</u>, Levy claimed, contrary to prevailing assumptions, that the framers of the First Amendment did not possess a libertarian concept of free speech or free press. Prior to publication of <u>Legacy of Suppression</u>, virtually all scholars followed the interpretation of the First Amendment espoused by Zecharia Chafee Jr. According to Chafee, the framers of the First Amendment had intended to wipe out the common law of sedition and to protect peaceful criticisms of government.[256]

In *Legacy of Suppression*, Levy concluded that Chafee was wrong and that the First Amendment did not reflect a libertarian ideology intended to eliminate the common law of seditious libel.[257] Levy argued that the libertarian theory at the time of the drafting of the First Amendment perceived no tension between protecting freedom of speech and punishing libels against the state, and that influential figures such as James Wilson embraced the distinction between prior restraint and subsequent punishment.[258] Consequently, according to Levy, the First Amendment did not intend to do away with the common law as taught by Blackstone. According to Blackstone, freedom of the press under the common law meant simply protection against restraint prior to publication: there was no protection subsequent to publication for seditious utterances.

In fact, during the colonial period the law of sedition was enforced widely.[259] Furthermore, it is well documented that many people at the time of the drafting of the Constitution viewed the term "freedom of the press" in the limited sense of an absence of prior restraint.[260] This was the Blackstonian interpretation. Indeed, Paine's definition of liberty of the press given in an 1806 newspaper piece was distinctly Blackstonian: "The term refers to the fact of printing free from prior restraint, and not at all to the matter printed, whether good or bad. The public at large--or in case of prosecution, a jury of the country--will be judges of the matter."[261]

In *Legacy of Suppression*, Levy argued that only after the Jeffersonians were forced to defend themselves against the Sedition Act of 1798 did a broad libertarian freedom of speech and press emerge in the United States. Once in power, however, the Jeffersonians became as intolerant of political criticism as the Federalists had been.[262]

In *Emergence of a Free Press*, Levy modified some of his original conclusions, particularly regarding the degree of actual press freedom in colonial America. Levy no longer believes that the history of political expression in America before 1800 reflects a legacy of suppression.[263] He now acknowledges that the press actually enjoyed remarkable freedom. In *Emergence*, Levy concedes that he was wrong in asserting that the American experience with freedom of political expression was as slight as the conceptual and legal framework was narrow: "from a far more thorough reading of American newspapers of the 18th Century, I now know that the American experience with the free press was as broad as the theoretical inheritance was narrow."[264] Levy, however, hedges his concession regarding the actual freedom of the press; he asserts that during the revolutionary era freedom of expression did not extend beyond contents approved by the majority. According to Levy, only the speech of freedom was free.[265]

Despite these revisions, however, Levy remains convinced that neither the American Revolution nor the First Amendment abolished the preexisting common law of seditious libel. Nor has Levy altered his view that the First Amendment is largely a lucky political accident whose scant theoretical foundation owed more to considerations of federalism than of libertarianism.[266] In examining the debate over the ratification of the Constitution and the Bill of Rights, Levy does not regard the First Amendment as an attempt to reform the prior law governing speech and the press. Instead, he views its development as part of the larger struggle between those favoring strong state or federal government and between federalists and antifederalists over the ratification of the Constitution.[267]

Levy admits to being puzzled and amazed that unfettered press practices occurred in a society which lacked a theory to justify those practices and which retained the law of seditious libel to punish them.[268] A central question posed in __Emergence of a Free Press__ is suggested by the paradox found by Levy: namely, the existence of "nearly unfettered press practices in a system characterized by legal fetters and the absence of a theory of political expression that justified those press practices."[269] In Levy's terms, freedom without a supporting theory, or freedom in spite of repressive theory and suppressive unenforced laws, was not truly freedom of expression. __Emergence of a Free Press__ reflects Levy's passionately held belief that the concepts of seditious libel and actual freedom of the press in practice cannot coexist.[270]

Despite his frequent assertion that the framers did not intend the First Amendment to change the common law, Levy occasionally acknowledges that it is impossible to determine their original understanding regarding the extent of constitutionally protected expression.[271] Levy states that

> "when the framers of the First Amendment provided that Congress shall not abridge the freedom of the press they could only have meant to protect the press with which they were familiar and as it operated at the time. They constitutionally guaranteed the practice of freedom of the press. They did not adopt its legal definition as found in Blackstone or in the views of libertarian theorists."[272]

Levy also states that the free press clause recognized and perpetuated an existing condition.[273] And he does conclude that the framers regarded a free press as a prerequisite to the republican government they desired.

These arguments by Levy support an historical analysis which looks to the role and conditions of the press at the time of ratification of the First Amendment to determine what the framers intended to protect. Furthermore, only the revised marketplace theory of the press clause can reconcile Levy's findings on seditious libel and the intent of the framers to protect in the First Amendment the type of free press that existed at the time.

CHAPTER III
THE CONTEMPORARY NEWSPAPER INDUSTRY

A. The Concentration of Media Ownership

A great discrepancy exists between the drafters' experience with the press and the reality existing today in the modern newspaper industry.[274] Indeed, the drafters of the First Amendment had no reason to anticipate a "marketplace of ideas" dominated by a few corporations in command of the mass media.[275] When the First Amendment was drafted and ratified, a true communications marketplace composed of numerous and independent presses existed, providing relatively easy access to the channels of communication.[276] The economics of the communications industry, however, has since concentrated the ability to participate in public debate into substantially fewer hands. Moreover, media concentration within particular geographic areas is especially severe.[277] Less than 4 percent of American cities have competing newspapers under separate ownership.[278] Thus, the free and independent American press has become a monopoly press.

Competition in the newspaper industry has greatly decreased in recent years. Although the total number of newspapers has not declined greatly, the number of communities with commercially competing daily newspapers under separate ownership has declined dramatically.[279] For instance, in 1910 there were 2,202 daily newspapers in 689 cities with commercially competing dailies; however, by 1968 those figures had dropped to 1,749 and 45 respectively.[280] From 1923 to 1973, the percentage of newspapers facing direct competition from another newspaper declined from sixty to five percent.[281] Furthermore, as media concentration has increased, newspaper publishing has also shifted from editor-ownership to corporate-ownership. In addition, the effective consolidation within the newspaper industry is magnified by the degree of intermedia ownership.[282] And there has occurred increasing intrusion of non-news corporations into the news enterprise. As of 1971, about one-half of the nation's daily newspapers were absentee-owned by corporate chains.[283] Today, two-thirds of the dailies are owned by chains.[284] Indeed, twenty corporations now control more than half the 61 million daily newspapers sold each day; and three corporations control most of the revenues and audience in television. According to Project Censored, a half dozen companies will control most of the news media by the 1990s.

In response to the growing concentration and power of the press, the public has become suspicious and reactionary toward advocacy of "freedom of the press." Public respect for the media has fallen in recent years, even in relation to other segments of society.[285] For instance, when the media complained that the Reagan Administration had prevented it from covering the Grenada invasion, most Americans sided with the government and believed that the media would not just report the invasion but would try to sabotage it.[286] Indeed, a growing public attitude of mistrust, as seen through the increasing number of libel suits and size of punitive damages awards against the press, displays a feeling that the public wants protections _from_ the press as well as protection _for_ the press.[287]

B. **Criticisms and Concerns Over Media Concentration**

Many critics view the concentration in the media industry as contradicting the spirit of the First Amendment by effectively creating a private censor.[288] Not only does concentration reduce the diversity of ideas expressed, it also makes widespread individual participation virtually impossible, substantially reduces face-to-face exchange of ideas, and creates an inequality of bargaining power in the communications marketplace.[289] Messages expressed by the modern media, contrary to those expressed by the colonial press, often are believed to be generally uncritical of the status quo.[290] In addition, and also contrary to the role of the early press, the modern mass media has the power to set the agenda for public discussion. According to Theodore White:

> "The power of the press is a primordial one. It sets the agenda of public discussion; and this sweeping political power is unrestrained by any law. It determines what people will talk about and think about--an authority that in other nations is reserved for tyrants, priests, parties and mandarins."[291]

The power of the modern media to shape the way our democracy operates is ever increasing.[292] Free and open debate on issues of public importance is necessary for the healthy functioning of a democracy. Yet as the power to shape opinion is concentrated in fewer hands, our democracy may grow less and less healthy.[293] Thus, concentration in the media industry threatens the democratic goal of pluralism.

The prevailing fear is that a pluralistic society can not function properly and continually with a large part of its population unable to access the media, unable to communicate and to organize with those of similar persuasion and interests, and unable to debate with and possibly convert those of differing views. Centralization of communications and denial of access to the media isolate the individual and discourage her responsible participation in public affairs.[294] Indeed, the Commission on Freedom of the Press, concluding that the modern press was not fulfilling its responsibility to society, warned that:

> "No democracy, certainly not the American democracy, will indefinitely tolerate concentration of private power irresponsible and strong enough to thwart the aspirations of the people."[295]

The Commission also found that, unlike the "bulletin board" role of the colonial newspapers, the owners of the modern press "determine which person, which facts, which version of the facts, and which ideas shall reach the public."

Grave doubts about traditional First Amendment precepts have arisen from the trend toward concentration and centralization in the communications media.[296] First Amendment theory has long been grounded on laissez faire concepts, as reflected by the durability of Holmes' marketplace of ideas metaphor. However, if the structure and economics of the modern press allow only a few to enter the marketplace, then the marketplace model no longer describes our system of communication; and a simple negative conception of the First Amendment as a protection against government interference no longer ensures diversity of expression.[297]

Along with the decline in diversity, concentration also decreases the number of persons able to participate in social communication. Contrary to the early American press, the modern media has become more than conduits of news and opinion, and no longer serves merely as middlemen between the events and the public. The modern media concentrated in a few corporations possesses the power to control access to the communications marketplace and selects the information entering the public dialogue. Therefore, as the communications media becomes ever more concentrated, centralized and remote, the public criticism of the press and the concern for the vitality of the marketplace of ideas concept rests largely on contemporary attitudes and reactions to the current patterns of media ownership.

The attack on the current state of media ownership rests upon several assumptions.[298] It is assumed that media ownership affects the content of the media message. This control sometimes occurs through overt censorship by the owners, but more often through subtle pressure on the editors and reporters. Under the traditional notion of a marketplace of ideas, diversity of views is inevitably linked to diversity of ownership of the media outlets through which those views are disseminated.[299] Consequently, many critics argue that concentrated ownership of media distorts a balanced presentation of ideas, since it is generally recognized that the point of view of media management, with some exceptions, tends to identify with the wealthy end of the economic spectrum.[300]

A second assumption underlying media ownership attacks holds that the media in the United States is becoming increasingly more concentrated in the hands of a few non-elected business executives or corporations and that such media concentrations will exercise unchecked political power.[301] According to a third assumption, concentration of corporate control over the media subverts local ownership, and hence responsiveness, of the media.[302] Chain journalism often involves centralized budget control in an excessively profit-conscious corporate headquarters far removed from the community a newspaper is seeking to serve. Excessive concentration of control over the media also increases the possibility of anti-competitive practices by media owners and of the possible domination of the mass media by self-serving economic interests.[303]

The courts have long been aware of the importance of a competitive media. They have vigilantly enforced the antitrust laws when dealing with the industry structure of the media. In so doing, the courts have acted to fulfill the First Amendment goal of achieving the widest possible dissemination of information from diverse and antagonistic sources.[304] The Supreme Court has stated that "a vigorous and dauntless press is a chief source feeding the flow of democratic expression and controversy which maintains the institutions of a free society."[305] Furthermore, the Court of Appeals for the District of Columbia, in recognizing the necessity of a free and competitive media, has stated that "it is also becoming increasingly obvious that application of antitrust doctrines in regulating the mass media is not solely a question of sound economic policy; it is also an important means of achieving the goals posited by the First Amendment."[306]

During his tenure on the Court, Chief Justice Burger was a strong critic of media concentration. In his concurring opinion in First National Bank of Boston v. Bellotti, he stated that "making traditional use of the corporate form, some media enterprises have amassed vast wealth and power and conduct many activities, some directly related--and some not--to their publishing and broadcasting activities."[307] The Chief Justice also recognized that:

> In Tornillo, for example, we noted the serious contentions advanced that a result of the growth of modern media empires has been to place in a few hands the power to inform the American people and shape public opinion.[308]

The widespread concern over the decline in competitive newspapers prompted Congress to enact the Newspaper Preservation Act (NPA) in 1970. Passed by overwhelming margins in both houses, the NPA allows two newspapers in a community--where one paper is failing--to combine their business and printing operations by entering into a joint operating agreement, so long as their editorial departments remain separate. The Act's supporters, recognizing that competing newspapers had gone out of business at an alarming rate, argued that the NPA was essential to preserve a diversity of editorial viewpoints. Indeed, of about 1,700 papers existing today, only thirty are competing. And with the recent failure of several large newspapers, particularly the St. Louis Globe-Democrat, the use and value of the NPA has received renewed attention.[309]

Recognizing the sharp decline in the number of daily newspapers, Owen argues that the spirit of the First Amendment implies a positive obligation of the government to intervene in various carefully defined ways when freedom of expression is threatened by private conglomerations of power.[310] He conceives of media firms as gatekeepers that control the flow of news and opinion and screen out ideas inimical to their economic interests or otherwise uncongenial to them.[311] Given this gatekeeper function, Owen argues that concentration in the media industries entails a reduction to dangerously low levels in the diversity of views disseminated to the public.[312] Thus, Owen's theory views the First Amendment as mandating a truly competitive media market, which in turn would produce a marketplace of diverse and competing ideas.

The loss of competitive newspapers, however, causes social concerns other than those relating to a loss of diverse viewpoints in the media. Newspapers give identity to the communities where they are published, and their disappearance somehow diminishes local civic spirit and morale.[313] Moreover, a diverse and competitive newspaper industry makes news management by the government more difficult. During World War II, for instance, the nation's newspapers proved the least malleable of the mass media. They were too numerous and too heterogeneous in outlook to fall easily into line.[314]

The increasing corporate conglomeration of the news media not only has drastically affected competition in the industry, but has changed the relationship between a newspaper and its subscribing community. Chain newspapers tend to become more responsive and subservient to their corporate owner than to the communities relying upon them for local news and public discourse. With 93 daily newspapers under its control, the Gannett chain is the largest newspaper chain in America and exemplifies some of the dangers associated with chain journalism. According to some critics, Gannett's replacement of community with corporate identity as the main focus of its newspapers illustrates the problems of chain ownership, since Gannett's corporate vision has little relevance to the particular needs or problems of the community in which one of its newspapers is located. In place of a fierce commitment to community that characterizes the best journalism, Gannett newspapers often employ generic front pages with a TV-like gloss that fits into the corporate vision.[315] The criticism of Gannett, as with the criticism of other large chains, is that serving the corporate culture and vision becomes more important to the editors than putting out a good community newspaper. According to critics, a single corporate vision is stamped on every newspaper in the chain; and, in achieving a generic-type newspaper, the typical Gannett paper devotes much more attention to features and sports than to news. What gets lost, unfortunately, is a community's distinctiveness and character.

CHAPTER IV

THE DIFFERENCES BETWEEN THE FREE SPEECH CLAUSE AND THE FREE PRESS CLAUSE

A. Introduction

A theory of the free press must address the widespread criticism currently levied against the modern press. It must also articulate and fulfill the values we place upon a free press in a democratic society. The revised marketplace model achieves both goals. It answers the public criticism surrounding the increased concentration in the press and the lack of diversity of opinions and citizen participation. At the same time, the revised marketplace model also fulfills the values that a free press should serve in a democratic society.

In constructing a First Amendment theory of the press clause, however, the initial inquiry must aim at distinguishing the speech and press clauses. To make this distinction, the particular values of a free press must be defined. The differences between the values of free speech and a free press will in turn suggest the different protections and functions of the two clauses.

Much of the current debate over the press clause revolves around whether the speech and press clauses protect different freedoms. This debate was fueled by Justice Stewart, when he suggested that there may be distinctive functions and features of "the press" that ought to be constitutionally protected by the Court.[316] Indeed, the First Amendment appears on its face to imply that "press" cases should not be treated as universally identical with "speech" cases in First Amendment litigation.[317]

The prevailing theories on the distinction between the press and speech clauses focus on whether the press should be treated the same or differently than the public.[318] Of those who think that the press should be treated differently, many adhere to the theory of the press as a "fourth estate" of government. The question, however, is whether one can accept a distinction between the press and speech clauses and yet not automatically follow the "fourth estate" model, which holds that the press primarily serves as an agent of the public to expose incidents of corruption in government and to fulfill the public's "right to know." The fourth estate model argues that the press clause contains a separate institutional or structural protection for the press, and thus confers different protections than those conferred by the speech clause.

Up to this point, the revised marketplace theory is in agreement with the fourth estate model. The differences between the two models will be seen in the nature of the press clause protections, which follow from the differences in the values and roles of a free press. Although both the revised marketplace and the fourth estate models conclude that the press clause is structural, the differing protections posited by each theory stem from a difference in the recognized values served by a free press.

The values of a free press often become obscured by an overly legalistic and technical approach to the press clause of the First Amendment. Yet constitutional protections should hinge upon what we really want to protect--a particular set of values associated with a free press. Currently, freedom of speech and press is determined to a significant degree by the identity of its actors and by its medium, rather than by the function and values of a free press. For instance, we regulate broadcasting in certain ways because of the medium by which it is circulated, even though in function it may have supplanted print as the primary source for news for most Americans and even though technology may have eliminated many of the original differences between print and broadcast media.[319]

Traditional First Amendment literature outlines several important functions served by free expression: (1) the development of the faculties of the individual and the promotion of self--expression; (2) the happiness derived from engaging in the activity of communication; (3) the provision of a safety valve for society; (4) the promotion of democratic government and society; and (5) the discovery and spread of political truth.[320] Justice Brandeis articulated these functions in his infamous concurring opinion in Whitney v. California.[321] Professor Blasi has more recently identified an important variant of the fourth and fifth values--the watchdog value of a free press.[322] Although most authors agree that any form of communication can potentially serve any one of these functions, and though most free press theories recognize this general mix of values, the essence of each theory of the press clause depends upon the relative weight given to each value.[323] For instance, Blasi's "watchdog value" forms the basis of the fourth estate model.

The construction of a free press constitutional theory therefore requires an identification of the broad values that a free press serves and achieves. The values discussed below apply to the press industry in general and differ from the functions of an individual newspaper, which will be discussed later, and also differ somewhat from the traditional approach as outlined by Justice Brandeis.

B. <u>The Values of a Free Press Under the Revised Marketplace Model</u>

1. <u>The Attainment of Truth From a Competition of Diverse Ideas</u>

The value of truth from the free expression of ideas was firmly recognized in political thought for more than a century preceding the adoption of the First Amendment. John Milton, for instance, wrote in protest of the English system of licensing that truth is best tested and falsehood best suppressed when they compete against each other through expression.[324] Later, the writings of John Stewart Mill strengthened the marketplace theory; and his essay <u>On Liberty</u> greatly influenced the development of basic First Amendment beliefs.[325] Mill advocated uninhibited expression as the best means for testing the truth of opinions, as well as for reinvigorating worthwhile beliefs.[326] Significantly, Mill did not advocate free expression for any intrinsic value: he advocated it as the best means of achieving a more fundamental goal--the spread of truth.[327]

American proponents of free expression at the time of the ratification of the Bill of Rights similarly believed that the value of uninhibited expression lay in the discovery of truth and in its contribution to the progress of humanity.[328] The Continental Congress expressed this conviction throughout the almost two-decade span preceding the adoption of the First Amendment. In its address to the people of Quebec, for instance, the Congress advocated freedom of the press on the ground that it promotes truth.[329]

Twentieth-century theorists have continued to articulate the truth value of free expression. Professor Chafee found that "one of the most important purposes of society and government is the discovery and spread of truth on subjects of general concern, (and that) this is possible only through absolutely unlimited discussion."[330] Though Alexander Meiklejohn's view of the objective of the First Amendment is more limited than Chafee's, he still relies on its connection to the attainment of truth. According to Meiklejohn, the framers enacted the constitutional protection of speech and press to ensure the dissemination of the kind of political truth required for reasoned self-government.[331]

The truth value underlying the First Amendment initially found its expression in constitutional law through the marketplace metaphor employed by Mr. Justice Holmes. A typical statement of his "marketplace of ideas" concept appears in Holmes' dissent in Abrams v. United States:

> But when men have realized that time has upset many fighting faiths, they may come to believe even more than they believe the very foundations of their own conduct that the ultimate good desire is better reached by free trade in ideas--that the best test of truth is the power of thought to get itself accepted in the competition of

the market and that truth is the only ground upon which their wishes safely can be carried out."[332]

In <u>Whitney v. California</u>, Justice Brandeis similarly stated that the First Amendment carries the assumption that free expression is indispensable to the "discovery and spread of political truth" and that the "greatest menace to people is an inert people."[333] The marketplace metaphor again reappeared in <u>Associated Press v. United States</u>, where the Supreme Court stated that the purpose of freedom of speech and press is to assure "the widest possible dissemination of information from diverse and antagonistic sources."[334]

For nearly three centuries, the value of a free press in promoting truth has been expressed by the marketplace of ideas metaphor made famous by Justice Holmes. However, this metaphor does not itself define the value and function of a free press; it only describes the means by which to achieve the value of truth. The marketplace of ideas metaphor has traditionally been used to describe the way in which a free exchange of ideas--through competition in the marketplace--can produce truth. The traditional marketplace metaphor has held that the attainment of truth therefore justifies in part our protection of speech, but it has not specified the type of press industry or activities protected by the First Amendment.

2. The Promotion of Representative Self-Government

This value relates closely to the truth value, since the promotion of truth inevitably leads to a more reasoned and effective government. Indeed, one principle of First Amendment interpretation receiving nearly universal agreement states that a primary purpose of the Amendment is to sustain the process of representative self-government so clearly created in the constitutional scheme.[335] The Supreme Court has also recognized this purpose as a primary function of free expression.[336] The Court has stated that the First Amendment "forbids the state from interfering with the communicative processes through which its citizens exercise and prepare to exercise their rights of self-government."[337] This view of the First Amendment recognizes that a society cannot intelligently make decisions required of a self-governing people unless all possible views bearing upon such decisions are expressed.

Though the relationship of freedom of speech and press to the political process lies at the core of the First Amendment, neither the Court nor First Amendment scholars have explored fully the implications of the important relationship between First Amendment guarantees and constitutionally established democratic political processes.[338] The proposed revised marketplace model attempts to fill this void, and posits a close relationship between the free press clause and our constitutional democratic processes. It does so by examining the role of a free press in supporting democratic government.

A free press aids in the promotion of self-government in two ways. First, it facilitates the formation of political majorities; and second, it promotes the rational and well-reasoned operation of government. Alexander Meiklejohn was one of the foremost advocates of the latter value of free press. According to Meiklejohn, the framers enacted the First Amendment to ensure the dissemination of truth necessary for enlightened self-government.[339] To Meiklejohn, a central purpose of the First Amendment, if not the exclusive purpose, is to sustain the process of representative self-government to which the Constitution is obviously committed.[340] Professor Meiklejohn viewed the self-government rationale as a function distinct from and superior to the truth function:

> The First Amendment is not, primarily, a device for the winning of new truth, though that is very important. It is a device for the sharing of whatever truth has been won. Its purpose is to give to every voting member of the body politic the fullest possible participation in the understanding of those problems with which the citizen of a self-governing society must deal.[341]

This self-government value, sometimes called the democratic dialogue function, is especially applicable to the press.[342] Communication through the press contributes more significantly to the democratic dialogue than does speech through other channels.[343] Moreover, of all the media forms, newspapers best achieve the democratic dialogue function. Newspapers, for instance, provide for the greatest degree of citizen participation. While anyone may publish his or her views in a newspaper, they probably do not have the seven million dollars needed to develop their own cable system.[344] Furthermore, it has been found that newspapers have more influence over voters' perceptions of issues than does television.[345]

Not only does a free press aid in the rational functioning of self-government, but it also promotes citizen participation in government and the formation of political groups and political majorities needed in a democracy. Political majorities cannot be formed, and majoritarian decisions cannot be made, without free and open dissemination of ideas. Professor Ely's process-view of the Constitution recognizes that the Constitution's main function is to allow groups to participate in forming coalitions so as to engage in the democratic process.[346] Democratic government requires not only free and well-informed debate concerning the issues, but also a system or forum whereby citizens can participate in the public discussion of issues and in the public communication process which leads to the formation of factions and groups. Therefore, separate from the function of "advancing knowledge and discovering truth," a free press provides for the participation in political decision-making by all members of society.[347]

The participatory value of the free press is illustrated by Professor Leonard in The Power of the Press. Leonard theorizes that the involvement of the press in political reporting and debate led to a coinciding development of democratic politics and political participation. He also argues that the creation of a Republican style of government did not necessarily create Democratic participation in that government. This latter achievement was left to the press.[348] Thus, Leonard theorizes that the nature of political reporting determined or at least significantly influenced the nature of American politics. In so doing, he demonstrates the political role of the press and of the connection between voting and communicating.

Leonard's history of the press shows that it plays a greater political role than that envisioned by advocates of the fourth estate model of the press. Moreover, Leonard also reveals the harm that can occur from a concentration of "fourth estate" functions of the press. When the press focuses less on transmitting information and achieving a free flow of ideas, and focuses more upon its role as an aloof critic and investigator, it can lose touch with the public and cause the public to turn away from politics by diminishing public involvement in the process of political communication.

The value of democratic participation articulated by Leonard and by Professor Emerson also carries beyond the political realm. It embraces the ability to participate in the building of the whole culture, and includes free social communication in religion, art, science and areas of human learning and knowledge. Furthermore, the process of open discussion promotes greater social cohesion, since people are more ready to accept decisions that go against them if they have a part in the decision-making process. Freedom of expression thus provides a framework in which the conflict necessary to the progress of society can take place without destroying the society. It is an essential mechanism for maintaining the balance between stability and change.

A free press allows, or should allow, a greater degree of cohesion and communication among members of political groups and between different political groups. This in turn brings more people into the democratic process. Indeed, a close connection exists between an open and freely competitive press and the promotion of democratic pluralism. According to Professor Pool, a large number of competitive media outlets would foster and encourage pluralism.[349]

Of all the types of modern media, newspapers provide for the greatest degree of citizen participation. This factor has led courts to conclude that newspapers and broadcast media cannot be equated and are constitutionally distinguishable. This conclusion has not been based strictly on the "natural monopoly" argument. Indeed, it has been recognized that, while the Supreme Court has rejected economic scarcity as a basis for the regulation of newspapers, the lack of any access requirements for newspapers simply "does not prevent a member of the general public from expressing his opinions in that same medium--in that case, print".[350]

3. The Promotion of Society and Culture Compatible with Democratic Government

Social bonds between individuals require a means or forum for those individuals to communicate. Apart from its relation to democratic government, free and open communication is essential for the formation and maintenance of a society. Society, in turn, is a prerequisite for self-government; and free communication is both the builder and the adhesive of society.

The distinction between society and government was also perceived by the framers.[351] According to their view, society promoted happiness because it was a positive unification of individual's affections, while government promoted happiness negatively because it restrained the vices of persons joined in society. And the press provided the primary forum and vehicle for the type of broad-based participatory communication needed for democratic society-building.

Law in a democracy arises from social interests.[352] Government cannot create those interests; instead, it responds to social interests. Yet its ability to respond depends upon the communication of those interests. Communication, therefore, not only articulates those interests but in fact forms and develops social interests.[353] Thus, government arises from society, which in turn arises from the free communication between individuals. The First Amendment serves to preserve these social and political foundations.

Freedom to communicate gives to individuals the ability to create a common, social world. As Hannah Ahrendt has noted, a "life without speech has ceased to be a human life because it is no longer lived among men. Communication affirms our reality, because we are perceived by others".[354] And "man is to be understood not as an isolated individual but as a person living in society."[355] Without speech as a mode of unity, according to Dr. Arendt, neither the reality of one's self nor of the surrounding world can be known. Communication, therefore, is essential for social interaction and unity. Indeed, the rise of the modern nation-state and the spirit of nationalism has occurred under the banner of improved communications.[356]

Freedom of communication provides the social cohesiveness necessary for a social structure to survive. Without free communication, individuals cannot form a society with sufficient social cohesion. Government, by itself, cannot produce social cohesion; but such cohesion is necessary to stabilize the political branch of society. Freedom of communication, therefore, constitutes a precondition of all forms of political organizations.[357] It gives individuals an absolute power to create a common world--a public realm--which forms a prerequisite to the political organization of society. Democratic government must come from what is common among its citizens. For the political to exist, however, the existence of both the private and social worlds must be insured; and without the protection of free expression that existence is impossible. The absence of free and open channels of communication obstructs the ability of individuals to form, and live in, society.

An all-encompassing constitutional theory of a free press should recognize the role played by a communications system in building a democratic culture and society. Although many First Amendment scholars have addressed the connection between the First Amendment and the maintenance of democratic government, few have examined the more complex but vital web of relationships between free expression, the nature of culture and society, and the health of democratic government. A number of twentieth-century writers, beginning with John Dewey, have concluded that the conditions for democracy must exist in a culture and society in order for democratic government to thrive. Dewey in fact theorized that political freedom could not be maintained without an existing culture of freedom. He argued that

> The relations which exist between persons, outside of political institutions, relations of communication, of science, art and religion affect daily associations, and thereby deeply affect the attitudes and habits expressed in government and rules of law ... Political institutions are an effect, not a cause. This complete of conditions which taxes the terms upon which human beings live together is summed up in the word "culture". The problem is to know what kind of culture is so free in itself that it conceives and begets political freedom as its accompaniment and consequence.[358]

Thus, while democratic government arises out of a democratic society and culture, free expression and open channels of social communication constitute an important ingredient of a democratic culture.[359] Indeed, in <u>The Cultural Pattern in American Politics</u>, Robert Kelley demonstrates the profound influence and impact of culture upon American politics.

According to Dewey, the problem of freedom and of democratic institutions "is tied up with the question of what kind of culture exists; with the necessity of free culture for free political institutions."[360] Dewey further wrote that:

> The problem of freedom of cooperative individualities is then a problem to be viewed in the context of culture. The state of culture is a state of interaction of many factors, the chief of which are law and politics, industry and commerce, the arts of expression and communication, and of morals,

> or the values men prize and the ways in which they evaluate them; and finally, though indirectly, the system of general ideas used by men to justify and to criticize the fundamental conditions under which they live, their social philosophy.[361]

Dewey strongly believed that the "ways of interaction" between human nature and cultural conditions are the first and fundamental element in understanding society and freedom and the resulting political institutions. He denied that democratic institutions automatically maintain themselves, or that they can be identified with fulfillment of prescriptions laid down in a constitution. The framers, according to Dewey, understood these strong cultural influences on political institutions.

Under Dewey's theories, free and open expression is one of those essential conditions to creating a free culture, which in turn will maintain a free and democratic political order. Dewey believed that democracy could exist only in a free social environment. A free, independent and open press constitutes a necessary ingredient for such an environment. Professor Levy, in studying early America and the remarkable freedom enjoyed by the colonial press, also found that colonial Americans regarded a free press as a necessity to a democratic government.[362]

The open exchange of ideas through a free press allows society to become aware of the necessary cultural conditions for the successful working of democratic forms. A free press also allows future generations to recognize which non-political causes might restrict or enhance democratic government. More than a formal political mechanism, democracy encompasses the way people regulate their relationships with others and with the state.[363] A free press, by facilitating social interchange, makes such relationships possible and constructive.

The structure of social communication reflects and influences the structure and development of society.[364] For instance, recent studies have demonstrated that the speed with which news travels possesses important social and political consequences. In particular, one scholar has explored the relationships between community cohesiveness and the speed of the communications within eighteenth century America.[365] On the average, news from even the remote corners of New England was published in all of the Southern colonies in less than one-third of the time required for the dissemination of news from London.[366] This communication system helped transform America from a dependent English colony into an independent community with a sense of self-identity. Furthermore, within the colonies, Philadelphia and New York appeared to have been quite efficient distribution centers of the news.[367] Thus, it is not surprising that these cities in turn became centers of political debate and activity during the revolutionary period.

A social value of a free press closely related to the democratic culture value lies in the safety valve function of the First Amendment.[368] This value is often termed the "social order" function. A free press serves a valuable safety valve or social order function by allowing minorities access to the social and political arena. In this way, minority groups are not completely shut out of the public sphere and political arena. Moreover, peaceful expression of these groups' views avoids the pent-up release of violent expression of those views.

Freedom of expression is a method of achieving a more adaptable yet more stable community. The opportunity and ability to communicate serves as a means through which to develop and maintain a facilitative social order.[369] Suppression of discussion, on the other hand, promotes inflexibility and prevents society from adjusting to changing circumstances and from developing new ideas. Furthermore, the process of open discussion through the press promotes greater cohesion in society because individuals are more ready to accept decisions that go against them if they have input into the decision-making process.[370]

Justice Brandeis, in his seminal opinion in <u>Whitney v. California</u>, also stressed the relationship between public order and free expression. For Brandeis, underlying the First Amendment are the assumptions that "it is hazardous to discourage thought, hope and imagination; that fear breeds repression; that repression breeds hate; that hate menaces stable government; and that the path of safety lies in the opportunity to discuss freely supposed grievances and proposed remedies."[371] Recently, it has been suggested that the contemporary threat to Brandeis' "path of safety" lies in the lack of opportunity for the disadvantaged and the dissatisfied of our society to discuss supposed grievances effectively.[372] Therefore, a further value of the safety valve function lies in the opportunity that freedom of speech gives to persons in power to learn about and respond to grievances before citizens become irretrievably alienated.[373]

4. **The Value of the Press in Acting as a Watchdog on Government**

A free press often alerts the public to abuses and incidents of corruption in government. This "watchdog" role is served when the press discovers and disseminates information about conditions otherwise kept from public view or which, if not hidden in a legal sense, are nonetheless unlikely to be discovered except by the press.[374]

Justice Stewart advocated a constitutional theory of the free press clause constructed primarily upon this "watchdog" value. According to Justice Stewart, the primary purpose of the free press clause is to create a "fourth estate" outside the government to serve as an additional check on the three official branches.[375] Justice Douglas also expressed this view when he stated that "the function of the press is to explore and investigate events, inform the people what is going on, and to expose the harmful as well as the good influences at work."[376]

Professor Blasi was one of the first advocates of the "watchdog" or checking value theory of the First Amendment press clause.[377] He viewed the First Amendment as protecting the value that free speech and free press can serve in checking abuses of power by public officials.[378] Blasi also saw this function and value as distinct from that of the self-governing rationale affected by Meikljohn.[379] However, under Blasi's theory, the public occupied a more passive role in the stream of political communication than it occupied under Meikljohn's theory. In Blasi's view, the role of the ordinary citizen is not so much to contribute on a continuing basis to the formation of public policy as to retain a veto power to be employed when the decisions of officials pass certain bounds.[380] This view, of course, contradicts the value of ongoing and constant citizen participation and decision-making--a value advanced by the "revised marketplace" theory.

Under the fourth estate theory, the press acts as an agent of the public, investigating and exposing government overreaching and corruption. The press occupies, in effect, a fourth branch so as to check the three official branches of government. To empower the press to fulfill such a role, "fourth estatists" argue that the press should have special rights of access and protection to gather news. Thus, a free press essentially equates with a "powerful press." While valuing oversight of governmental actions, however, the revised marketplace, as discussed further below, does not elevate the press to a specially-appointed role as public agent. Nor does it envision the granting of special privileges to an already concentrated press as essential to the functioning of a free press in a democratic society.

Not surprisingly, the "watchdog" or "fourth estate" theory of the press followed in the wake of the shift toward adversary journalism that took place in the 1960s.[381] This shift toward adversarial or investigative journalism intensified during the Vietnam War and the Watergate scandal. During that time, the press became deeply antagonistic and combative toward a government perceived to be secretly acting against the interests of the American public.[382]

C. **The Separate Values Protected by the Speech and Press Clauses of the First Amendment**

1. Introduction

Professor Nimmer, having concluded that it is possible to distinguish between press and speech activities, posed the question as to whether the freedom of the press should differ substantially from that accorded to speech.[383] Although Nimmer attempted to explore this question, he admittedly only begun the inquiry. To pick up where Nimmer left off necessitates a broader inquiry into the different values served by free speech and a free press, and whether separate constitutional protections are required to guard those different values.

A determination of whether the press clause confers protections or rights separate from those granted by the speech clause requires an identification of separate values protected by the press and speech clauses. Although Professor Emerson has outlined the broad ideals and values of a system of free expression, a similar framework has yet to be outlined regarding the separate natures and values of a constitutional protection of free speech and a free press. Under the revised marketplace theory, the speech and press clauses confer different constitutional protections. In summary, the speech clause assures to each individual the freedom to speak and the freedom from any state sanction based upon the content of that speech. The press clause, however, addresses the dissemination of those views in society and assures an open forum for communication in society and for democratic political participation. Thus, the press clause does not merely protect individuals in the act of printing or broadcasting their ideas--the speech clause adequately serves that purpose.

While the speech clause protects individuals in their act of speaking, the press clause protects the system of dissemination of those views. In effect, the distinction is one between free speech and the conditions necessary for its expression. Professor Schauer, in Free Speech: A Philosophical Inquiry, recognizes this distinction.[384] He notes the vexing problem of private censorship and the relation of the right of free speech to the ability to speak. The revised marketplace model addresses this concern and holds that the free press clause protects the maintenance of conditions conducive for the diverse public expression of ideas.

2. The Separation of Individualistic and Societal Values in the First Amendment.

One difference between the speech and press clauses lies in their differing application to the value of individual autonomy and dignity. Individual free expression, protected by the free speech clause, preserves the individual's dignity and autonomy.[385] This self-fulfillment function of speech finds little counterpart in relation to the press, especially given the corporate makeup of the media.[386] While the free speech clause rests upon the view that society must respect individual autonomy as an end in itself, the press clause is directed more to the dissemination of individual speech in society and to the nature of the institutions that disseminate that speech.[387]

Justice Powell's opinions illustrate this distinction between the individual and social values underlying the two classes and show that we can find differing protections granted by the speech and press clauses even though we do not adopt Justice Stewart's "fourth estate" role for the press. In his dissent in Saxbe v. Washington Post Company[388] and his opinion in First National Bank v. Bellotti,[389] Justice Powell espoused a process-protective, societal function of the First Amendment. Citing Professor Chafee's observation that the guarantees of freedom of speech and press protect two kinds of interests, Justice Powell distinguished between the individualistic values served by the First Amendment and the societal function of the First Amendment in preserving free public discussion of government affairs.[390] Chafee had likewise envisioned the First Amendment as protecting two kinds of interests: the interest of individuals to express their opinions, and the social interest in the attainment of truth.[391]

Employing Justice Powell's distinction, the revised marketplace theory posits that the individualistic and societal values of the First Amendment coincide with the speech and press clauses respectively, and that the societal function relates to the maintenance of an open, easily accessible and competitive press industry. The individual operations and publications of particular media organizations are then protected by the speech clause.

The speech clause of the First Amendment, though primarily concerned with preserving individual liberty, also serves to enhance the democratic process. However, the value to democratic government does not alone justify the free speech clause. That clause is based upon a respect for individual rights and dignity. The free press clause, on the other hand, more directly focuses on the public interest in promoting democratic society and government. Indeed, the public interest provides the ultimate justification for press rights.[392] The press clause therefore focuses more on providing a forum or marketplace for individual speech than in protecting the act of speaking and the content of the particular speech. While the speech clause focuses on the individual, the press clause focuses upon the dynamics and source of that speech in society and upon the communication forum in which that speech is expressed.

The "societal" interpretation of the press clause essentially focuses on a literal view of the First Amendment language. The Amendment protects the act of speaking. This protection extends to actors who are capable of speaking. The First Amendment also protects "the press". This protection extends to preserving a marketplace or forum made up of competitive and independent press entities. Insofar as the press discharges this societal function, it is entitled to First Amendment protection.

The societal function protects the political process by preserving free public discussion of governmental affairs.[393] It follows from the First Amendment's concern with democratic processes:

> No aspect of that Constitutional guaranty of the First Amendment is more rightly treasured than its protection of the ability of our people through free and open debate to consider and resolve their own destiny . . . the First Amendment is one of the vital bulwarks of our national commitment to intelligent self-government.[394]

The significance of distinguishing claims related to the process-protective, societal function of the First Amendment from those based upon its individualistic values lies in accepting the distinction between the speech and press clauses and the values served by each clause.

Viewed from the societal function perspective, the First Amendment press clause seeks to protect the public's interest in the integrity of an ongoing social and political process.[395] Rather than approaching the press clause as a protection of certain specific individual rights or activities, the revised marketplace theory views it as a broader protection of certain aspects of the democratic process and the communicative process which leads to self-government. Thus, the theory answers in the affirmative the question posed by Professor Nimmer: May there be an abridgement of the First Amendment guarantees of free press if the individual act of communication in itself is subject to neither prohibition, punishment or other penalty?[396]

Justice Brennan's opinions also suggest that the First Amendment affords protection not only for communication itself, but for the indispensable conditions of meaningful communication.[397] This two-part view reflects the speech and press distinction under the revised marketplace theory. Justice Brennan's first protection involves free speech while the latter protection involves free press. Since a free and competitive marketplace of independent presses may constitute one indispensable condition of meaningful communication, the First Amendment press clause therefore protects the social channels of communication rather than specific utterances or specific rights of the press to conduct its day-to-day operations, which are protected by the speech clause. Thus, the societal function of the First Amendment is found in the press clause and is served by the maintenance of a communications forum made up of an open and competitive press.

3. <u>The Free Press Clause as a Positive Liberty</u>

Two prominent themes have influenced the judicial and philosophical justifications for free speech and free press. One emphasizes the role of free speech in individual self-expression and in the development of individual potential; whereas the other stresses the value of free expression to a system of self-government.[398] The individual self-expression theme sees the First Amendment as ensuring an inviolable private sphere of liberty to the individual. The second theme employs the First Amendment to protect the positive functioning of democratic government.

Isaiah Berlin has labeled the first theme or concept of liberty as a negative freedom--an individual's freedom from government interference.[399] The latter theme Berlin defines as a positive concept of liberty. This liberty constitutes the right to self-government or, more accurately, the power to self-govern. Berlin separated liberty of expression from the issue of self-government. According to Berlin, the answer to the questions "who governs me?" is logically distinct from the questions "how far does government interfere with me?"[400] Berlin's two concepts of freedom apply separately to the speech and press clauses respectively.

Under Berlin's theory, the free press clause protects a positive liberty while the free speech clause protects a negative liberty. Consequently, the free speech clause inures solely to the individual, while the free press clause serves as a positive liberty essential for self-government. The press clause can be seen as protecting a forum which connects the desires and needs of society with the actions of democratic government. Indeed, without such a forum, a society could not govern itself. The speech clause, however, protects that essential personal freedom which we must have if we are not "to degrade or deny our nature."[401]

Berlin's theories illustrate a basic distinction between the press and speech clauses that many jurists do not recognize. Modern First Amendment scholars such as Alexander Meiklejohn and Robert Bork argue that the First Amendment has value only in its relation to self-government and is, in effect, a positive liberty.[402] These authors, however, do not recognize the distinction between the speech clause and the press clause, and that one serves as a positive liberty while the other serves as a negative liberty.

The First Amendment, in Meiklejohn's view, protects the presence of self-government.[403] Meiklejohn argues that the First Amendment is not concerned with a private freedom to speak; it protects only the freedom of those expressions by which we govern. Meiklejohn's theory of the First Amendment is closely intertwined with his theory of self-government. Meiklejohn would give First Amendment protection only to those activities which are necessary for self-government. He views the First Amendment only in its relation to self-government. Meiklejohn's use of the First Amendment to protect activities only of governing importance indicates that he views the First Amendment as protecting a positive liberty. In Meiklejohn's theory, the First Amendment exists primarily as a power by which people can effectively govern themselves.

Bork adopts Meiklejohn's theory concerning the connection between self-government and the First Amendment. Like Meiklejohn, Bork takes a positive liberty view of the entire First Amendment, but does not distinguish between the speech and press clauses. Bork views the First Amendment as guarantying derivative rights--rights derived from the governmental processes established by the Constitution. Bork agrees with Meiklejohn in that the First Amendment does not protect a freedom to speak; rather it protects the freedom of those activities of communication by which we govern.[404] Thus, with Bork as with Meiklejohn, the First Amendment is concerned not with a private right, but with a public power. However, according to the revised marketplace model, the theories of Meiklejohn and Bork apply only to the free press clause of the First Amendment and not to the free speech clause.

The Court likewise has also confused the negative and positive liberties contained in the First Amendment. For instance, in Globe Newspaper Company v. Superior Court, where the Supreme Court clarified the right of access, Justice Brennan reasoned that the First Amendment protection of speech serves to ensure effective individual participation in our republican system of self-government.[405] The decision in Globe Newspaper illustrates the lack of clear distinctions in the Court's First Amendment theories between press and speech protections and the values and functions of each protection.

The revised marketplace theory seeks to clarify the differences between the press and speech clauses and to reconcile the theories of Berlin and Meiklejohn. Under this theory, the press clause protects the political process and communicative process necessary for self-government. It argues that the framers created a negative liberty in the speech clause and a positive liberty in the press clause.[406] Thus, the press clause deals with the public's right and ability to self-govern, while the speech clause deals with private rights of the individual. The press clause does not protect the freedom of an individual to print; it protects that forum through which individuals can effectively communicate as a society. Accordingly, the press clause of the First Amendment expresses a positive liberty needed by the public to form society and participate in self-government.

Under the revised marketplace theory, the press clause does not focus on the content of the communications. Rather, it focuses on providing a social channel for communications among citizens and between society and government. The marketplace metaphor is useful in that it describes the type of forum needed to provide for expression of diverse opinions and to provide for widespread social participation in the communicative and political process. Unlike previous definitions of the marketplace metaphor, the revised marketplace model does not focus on a beneficial side-effect--the attainment of truth from diverse speech--which occurs as a result of free expression. Indeed, the traditional marketplace metaphor used the marketplace concept to justify free speech. The revised marketplace model, however, does not use the marketplace model to merely justify a system of free expression. Instead, it envisions the marketplace metaphor as actually describing the dictates of the free press clause--i.e., the existence of an independent, freely accessible and competitive industry of newspapers--and interprets the press clause as providing the actual channels needed for open communication in a democratic society.

The First Amendment theories of Professor John Hart Ely also support the view that the free press clause protects a positive liberty. Professor Ely argues that the Constitution focuses primarily on concerns of process and structure and not on the identification and preservation of specific substantive values.[407] The First Amendment, according to Ely, serves to support the functioning of governmental processes and to ensure the open and informed discussion of political issues.[408] Ely contends that freedom of expression constitutes a critical ingredient for the proper functioning of an open and effective democratic process. He also argues that constitutional rights are devices for reinforcing the representation of positions and groups that are likely to be excluded from the majoritarian political process, and that judicial review should function only to strengthen the democratic process.[409]

Ely's view of the Constitution incorporates a positive liberty view of the press clause. Indeed, without a free press, political groups could not even begin communicating between themselves and with the rest of society. As Ely recognizes, the political process begins not at the ballot box but at the point where groups begin identifying political issues and communicating together. Although the free speech clause allows people to exercise their individual freedom to speak, the free press clause protects the process whereby those ideas come together in a social forum and marketplace so that the political process can begin.

4. **The Analogy of the Press Clause to the Establishment of Religion Clause**

The speech and press clauses can be analogized to the religious exercise and establishment clauses of the First

Amendment. The speech clause, like the free exercise clause, protects the individual's negative liberty. Conversely, the press clause, like the establishment clause, protects the public interest in a particular structure of nongovernmental or cultural aspects of society. While the establishment clause governs the relationship between religion and government, the press clause governs the relationship between speech in society, an open and competitive communication forum, and the political process.

First Amendment scholars have likewise suggested that the establishment of religion clause in the First Amendment provides a helpful analogy to use in understanding the press clause.[410] They recognize that both the establishment clause and the press clause protect the independence and integrity of vital nongovernmental centers of expression and power.[411] Thus, by analogy, we can interpret some First Amendment clauses (free exercise and speech) as focused on individual liberty, and others (the establishment and press clauses) as focused on principles that apply to the relation between government and specific institutions existing in society.[412]

D. The Free Press Guaranty: A Structural Provision of the Constitution

The free speech clause protects individuals in the act of speaking and communicating. Its protection inures to the individual and, as such, constitutes an individual right or liberty. The press clause, on the other hand, does not focus strictly on individual rights and liberties. Contrary to contemporary First Amendment theories, the revised marketplace theory holds that the press clause does not merely protect individuals in the act of printing or broadcasting their ideas: indeed, the free speech guaranty adequately protects the content of speech, whether the words be spoken or printed. Therefore, since the press clause does not just protect individual rights, it must be seen as a broader protection--a structural provision of the Constitution. This structural aspect of the press clause arises from its attachment to the press as an industry and social communication forum, rather than to specific individual activities.

Justice Stewart has recognized the structural feature of the press clause and has advocated this view in First Amendment adjudication:

> Most of the other provisions in the Bill of Rights protects specific liberties or specific rights of individuals . . . in contrast, the free press clause extends protection to an institution. The publishing business is, in short, the only organized business that is given explicit constitutional protection.[413]

According to Justice Stewart, the free press guaranty would be a constitutional redundancy if it meant no more than freedom of expression. Yet while Justice Stewart extends institutional protection to the press, he extends that protection for the primary purpose of creating a "fourth institution outside the government as an additional check on the three official branches."[414]

Several Supreme Court opinions have recognized Stewart's structural view of the press clause. In Gertz v. Robert Welch, Inc., the Court relied on institutional considerations and processes unrelated to specific content.[415] The Court continued to stress a structural role in Richmond Newspapers, Inc. v. Virginia.[416] As Justice Brennan stated, "the First Amendment embodies more than a commitment to free expression and communicative interchange for their own sakes: it has a structural role to play in securing and fostering our republican system of self-government."[417]

While the Court's previous use of the structural view has focused on the role of the press as an adversarial check on government--the watchdog function--a structural analysis can also be applied by the revised marketplace model to the free press clause. Such an analysis would focus upon protecting the structure of a competitive and independent press easily accessible to the public.

Professor Pool, for instance, adopts a structural view and argues for an open and competitive press. His structural view advocates government regulation over the media only to the extent that a particular media actually is monopolized.[418] By advocating government regulation only when a monopoly exists, Pool argues that our communication mediums should be decentralized, dispersed and competitive.[419] Thus, Pool takes a structural approach and accords constitutional protection only to an open and competitive press. A press characterized by monopoly conditions, on the other hand, does not receive protection and, as Pool argues, should be subject to governmental regulation.[420]

The actual language of the First Amendment also weighs in favor of interpreting the press clause as an institutional or structural protection. The Amendment protects speech and the press. Speech is the product of speaking, and the Amendment's protection extends to actors who are capable of speaking. The Amendment's reference to the press, however, is an institutional reference. The press is not the product of any verb; it is a noun connoting a physical entity.[421] Historical evidence also supports this interpretation. For instance, in his draft Constitution for Virginia, Thomas Jefferson proposed the following language: "Printing presses shall be free..."[422] Jefferson's reference to "printing presses" is to a physical entity--a means of communicating.

As the revised marketplace model demonstrates, it is possible to adopt a structural analysis of the free press clause while not accepting Justice Stewart's fourth estate model. In his theory, Justice Stewart contends that the framers intended to protect a fourth estate function of the press. It is more likely, however, that the framers intended to protect a competitive press which served as a marketplace of ideas. Throughout the formative period, the focus of discussion was on the political role of the press and its relation to self-government.[423] The structural aspect of the press clause derived from the framer's desire to preserve the type of press industry with which they were familiar, not to protect the role of the press as an institutional ombudsman or agent of the public, as envisioned by the fourth estate model.[424] Therefore, as outlined in the revised marketplace theory, concluding that the press clause is structural in nature does not require an adoption of the fourth estate model.

    E.   <u>The Historical Basis for Interpreting the Press Clause as a Structural Provision of the Constitution</u>

An historical discussion of the actual conditions and circumstances surrounding the colonial and revolutionary press reveals some of the intent and meaning underlying the free press clause--if we assume that the framers would have wanted to protect the type of press industry that had existed during the colonial and revolutionary periods. We cannot know for sure whether the framers would have acted differently if they had been faced with a media structure such as we have today. However, the evidence shows that their experience was with a highly opinionated and competitive press and with one in which there was great accessibility.

The historical analysis of the early American press yields several conclusions. First, a very competitive and open press existed during the colonial and revolutionary eras. There was easy access to printing presses, and new presses could start up fairly easily. Both the presses and printers were relatively mobile. Thus, with low barriers of entry to the printing industry, the number of newspapers constantly increased. Furthermore, presses were relatively small-scale and were very sensitive to the communities' ideas and demands.

Second, newspaper publishers and editors, especially in the late colonial and revolutionary period, viewed their role as a political one. They also recognized their role in uniting the colonies. Editors believed that their papers were to serve as forums in which to air political debate. Therefore, the contents of the newspapers tended to focus primarily on political opinion essays contributed by subscribers, and not on "hard news" and investigative reporting. Indeed, the newspapers were not supposed to act just as investigative bodies digging up facts. Political opinion constituted an important part of the early newspapers. As evidence of the importance of opinion-publishing, there was a distinct tendency to print propaganda pieces over objective reporting. In this vein, newspapers served a central role in providing a channel of communication among society and between the colonies for the expression of opinions.

Third, the physical makeup of a colonial printing press also supports the idea of the press clause as a "marketplace protector". Printers set up printing presses which essentially served as bulletin boards for the community. Printers were viewed as "mechanics," and only much later as "partisans" also. The printer did not have a staff to investigate and report stories. Instead, the printer was dependent upon the community for providing news or opinions to place in the newspaper. For instance, despite the increased power of the press during the Revolutionary period, Schlesinger concludes that it had never been anything more than a mere transmitter of public opinion.[425] In effect, the duty of the printer was to provide the physical means for society to communicate. Furthermore, the historical evidence shows that one newspaper could not present all the viewpoints of the community-- several newspapers were needed to do that.

Fourth, the reaction to the type of restrictions placed upon colonial and revolutionary newspapers casts in doubt the fourth estate model of the press. Newspapers opposed both the British Stamp Act and the proposed postal restrictions in 1792. Both these measures in effect placed a tax upon the circulation and dissemination of newspapers. Printers had also protested the licensing system which had been brought over from Britain. Perhaps the strongest colonial argument against licensing was that the licensing system perpetuated monopolies in the printing press industry.

Protests over these restrictions demonstrate that Americans wanted a free and competitive newspaper industry. Also, the free circulation of newspapers appears to have been more important to them than freedom from persecution for seditious libel. The framers seemed to be more concerned about getting ideas out into the public than about the particular content and quality of those ideas. For instance, colonial and revolutionary newspapers tended to print rumor and emotional propaganda. However, as long as there were enough newspapers to permit a full array of ideas to circulate among the public, the publication of some rumor and propaganda did not seem to pose a problem for the framers. They seemed more concerned with having outlets for publishing their own ideas rather than ensuring that whatever ideas were printed were of a particular quality or content. There did occur in some sectors of the press a reasoned examination of some of the underlying problems and issues of imperial relations;

generally, however, the newspapers did not focus on a reasoned and rational approach but rather merely espoused the patriot cause.

The framers' tolerance and encouragement of an opinionated press contradicts the fourth estate model. The fourth estate model is also not supported by the historical fact that when the Continental Congress met in Philadelphia in 1774, all delegates agreed that for the time being no news should be leaked to the press.[426]

Levy's thesis on the existence of the law of seditious libel does not affect the validity of the revised marketplace model of the free press clause. Under this model, the free press clause was designed to protect the structure of the newspaper industry rather than the content of the particular speech, which was addressed by the speech clause. This model even is consistent with the status of the common law of seditious libel. The revised marketplace model can be harmonized with an intent of the framers to retain the common law of seditious libel, since the marketplace of ideas model does not focus on the content of the speech and does not perceive the press as a watchdog on government. In effect, seditious libel seemed to be more of a political question to the framers than a constitutional question. For instance, the protests of the press over that law did not result from a belief in principle but simply from whatever instances of prosecutions faced an editor at the particular time. Thus, some editors favored prosecutions for seditious libel at some times and not at other times. However, they all protested restrictions on a competitive press industry, such as the Stamp Act, the licensing system and the postal rate increases.

Even if Levy's research is correct in that actual freedom of the press during the revolutionary era did not extend beyond the contents approved by the majority, this proposition does not affect the revised marketplace theory. The framers could have fully realized this role in drafting the First Amendment, yet could have inserted the free press clause to address the industry aspects of the press rather than the particular content of the views contained in the newspapers. Thus, the framers could have realized the role that the press played in the Revolution and wanted to continue the particular structural aspects of the press. Furthermore, Levy's conception that the First Amendment was part of a larger struggle between Federalists and anti-Federalists, rather than an attempt to reform the prior law governing speech and the press, supports a theory that the press clause had more to do with the relations between society and government than upon the regulations governing content of speech.

CHAPTER V

THE APPLICATION OF THE REVISED MARKETPLACE MODEL
TO THE FUNCTIONS OF THE PRESS

A. Introduction

The revised marketplace model serves the values of a free press through a two-part approach. First, it affords protection to each individual media outlet for the performance of that individual media's press and speech functions. This protection can be analogized to a negative liberty--whereby a newspaper is given protective status to carry out its functions, but is not given any special affirmative rights. This individual protection also involves essentially a free speech protection for the media entity. The second aspect of the model addresses the structure of the press industry. Unlike the fourth estate model, however, it does not create an independent activist entity to perform certain "governmental" or "checking" functions. Instead, the revised marketplace model looks at the physical makeup of the press industry and tries to achieve two primary goals: first, media responsiveness to the community and diversity of expression; and second, wide public participation in the society-building and self-government processes.

The traditional approach to the media functions protected by the free press clause looks only to the functions of an individual newspaper, not to the overall structural or industry-wide aspects of the press. The revised marketplace model takes a broader view. Under this model, the free press clause protects an institutional framework of independent, competing newspapers that provide opportunities for participation, community responsiveness and an accessible forum to speakers. The scope of the revised marketplace model can be analyzed from a two-tiered analysis of the functions and features of a free press: first, an outline of those functions which are essential for an individual newspaper to perform; and second, a discussion of those functions and features of the institutional structure of a free press composed of independent and competing newspapers.

The difference between the fourth estate model and the revised marketplace model is that the former creates a privileged industry while the latter protects a competitive one. Under the revised marketplace model, the press does not represent the public or act as an agent of society in its dealings with government. Rather, the press acts as a channel for communications to pass through society and from society to government. The revised marketplace model obviously puts high emphasis on the democratic value of citizen participation in the communications process, on the idea that natural communications within society must exist so that government can develop from a cohesive society, and on the social importance of shared public opinions as compared with a one-way communication of investigative facts.

B. **The Functions of an Individual Newspaper Protected as Negative Liberties**

Under the revised marketplace model, individual newspaper organizations receive a type of constitutional protection different from the type of structural protection accorded to the newspaper industry as a whole. However, a definition of the constitutional protections granted to an individual newspaper requires a specification of the basic and necessary functions of an individual newspaper. Adequate protection must then be given to each one of those necessary functions.

The traditional approach to cases involving the free press clause calls for the protection of three distinct media functions.[427] First, the media must have the ability to collect information. This function, often referred to as "the newsgathering function", requires access to information as well as the ability to ensure that the sources of the information collected will remain confidential. The second major function performed by media outlets is the editorial function. This involves analysis of the information collected and the decision-making process as to the content and form in which the news will appear. The third function is the publication and distribution of information.

Although protection of each function rests upon the same constitutional phrase--the free press clause--the Supreme Court has imposed varying constitutional standards for each. The Court has never explicitly recognized the interrelationship of the three functions, nor has it developed a consistent free press theory incorporating the various press functions.[428] The revised marketplace model, however, defines an overall free press theory in terms of the vital functions of a free press, even though those protected functions and values are somewhat different and broader than the traditional analysis. Furthermore, protections conferred by the revised marketplace model apply consistently to each press function outlined above.

The writing and editing component currently receives almost absolute protection from government interference.[429] Government may never dictate what information must or cannot be included in a story or how that information must be arranged.[430] Professor Schmidt, for instance, argues that the Court has protected the principle of publisher autonomy not as a means of achieving the maximum possible diversity of expression but rather as an end in itself.[431] Likewise, although the revised marketplace model concludes that the editing function would be a value under the free speech clause and protected by the free speech clause as a negative liberty, an independent editorial decision-making process is also necessary for the free press clause. Otherwise, a press organization would not fit the model of an independent organization in a diverse and competitive industry structure. As the Court in <u>Tornillo</u> argued, a newspaper is more than a passive receptacle or conduit for news and advertising.[432] Indeed, the early American newspapers were very partisan organizations. Furthermore, editorial independence is necessary to preserve speech rights of those persons speaking through the particular media organization.

The publication component also receives a high level of protection, but additional restrictions on press activity appear at this point. For instance, publishers may be liable for civil damages for invasion of privacy[433] or for libel.[434] In short, the publication component does not receive absolute protection, but governmental restrictions on publishing may withstand constitutional scrutiny only if they serve a significant societal interest and only if they do not directly or indirectly impair the basic functions of the press.

The level of constitutional protection diminishes substantially, however, for the distribution component. Although government may not prohibit distribution of information,[435] reasonable regulations regarding the time, place and manner of distribution are permissible. This standard reflects the general view that freedom of expression grants more protection to pure expression than it does to conduct,[436] and that distribution is primarily conduct.[437]

Protection of the dissemination and publication function allows the press industry to serve as a marketplace of competitive and independent sources of information. Dissemination and publication is the point at which ideas actually enter the marketplace and are communicated to society. Freedom of the press would be of little value if newspapers could not be freely circulated. The Supreme Court has recognized that "liberty of circulating is as essential to [freedom of the press] as liberty of publishing; indeed, without the circulation, the publication would be of little value."[438] Indeed, some courts have viewed infringements on dissemination as constituting a prior restraint.[439] Moreover, several recent decisions have even indicated that the Court values the dissemination function over the access or newsgathering function. In <u>Seattle Times Co. v. Rhinehart</u>[440] and in <u>U.S. v. Smith</u>,[441] the U. S. Supreme Court, although limiting press access to certain confidential information, recognized that the press could not be prohibited from publishing that same information if it could be obtained from other sources.

Of the four functions performed by each press entity, the newsgathering function commands the least constitutional protection. The newsgathering function has only recently received independent constitutional protection.[442] Not until 1972 did the constitutional right to gather news come before the Supreme Court in <u>Branzberg v. Hayes</u>.[443] Although the Court recognized that newsgathering was entitled to some constitutional protection, the plurality opinion narrowly restricted that protection. At the present time, however, the Court has not yet developed a consistent stance toward a right of newsgathering. While the Court has recognized a First Amendment right to gather news, it has refused to enforce it in various situations.[444]

The right of newsgathering has been extensively discussed and debated, especially by "fourth estate" advocates. Generally, those espousing a right of newsgathering usually assert that such a right gives the press a right of access to government information. For instance, in the <u>Pell</u> and <u>Saxbe</u> cases, the litigants argued that they should be able to obtain access to state and federal prisons. It was not, however, until <u>Richmond Newspapers, Inc. v. Virginia</u>, that the Court expressly invoked the right to gather information.[445] The <u>Richmond</u> decision, which produced no opinion on behalf of the Court, was followed by Globe Newspaper Company v. Superior Court,[446] which invalidated a Massachusetts statute excluding the press and general public from the testimony of a minor victim in a sex offense trial. In Globe, the Court based its opinion on the general right to gather information recognized in Richmond.[447]

The reporter's privilege also may be viewed as a logical corollary of the right to gather information.[448] However, in Branzberg v. Hayes--the only Supreme Court decision to date which has squarely ruled upon the issue of the confidentiality of informants--the majority opinion denied the asserted privilege.[449] Nonetheless, the Branzberg majority did concede that the privilege should withstand inquiries not made in good faith.[450] Thus, a privilege of the press as to the identity of its sources is grounded in the First Amendment right to gather information. It is only because the absence of such a qualified privilege would deter the press' independent ability to gather information that the privilege itself has a constitutional base. Advocates of this privilege have argued that the absence of such a privilege would dry up the sources of information, creating a barren marketplace with no meaningful information to exchange.[451]

Newsgathering, like the editorial, publication and dissemination functions of an individual newspaper, should be protected as a negative liberty--and not in an affirmative manner as espoused by the fourth estate model. Under the revised marketplace model, all of the individual functions of a press entity receive equal and consistent protection in the form of a negative liberty. According to the negative liberty view, the press clause prohibits government from actively infringing upon a newspaper's ability to gather, edit and circulate news. It does not, however, grant to the press affirmative rights that are unavailable to the public. Thus, the government is not obliged to promote the individual activities of the press, nor to give special privileges to the press which are unavailable to the public. The Court has upheld this lack of special privilege in the Pell and Saxbe cases.

Most jurists who espouse affirmative protection for newsgathering as a "positive liberty" also view the press according to the "fourth estate" model.[452] They believe that the press should act as a governmental watchdog and, for example, should be allowed to go into a prison and to conduct its own investigation of that prison. Under the fourth estate theory, investigative reporting receives a higher priority than opinion dissemination. Thus, it is obvious to see that if one holds the fourth estate model, one must also hold that an affirmative right of newsgathering is vital to a free press. This view, however, marks a crucial distinction between the fourth estate model and the revised marketplace model. Under the latter theory, the press does not act as a quasi-organ of government, but rather as a forum which permits and facilitates communication among society. Thus, the press performs its function when it publishes opinions about why a prison does not allow access.

Those who argue for an affirmative protection of newsgathering emphasize investigative reporting over opinion dissemination. This emphasis marks another important distinction between the fourth estate and revised marketplace models.

Opinion dissemination deserves greater constitutional protection, since it allows for a greater political participation by the public. The press does not constitute a branch of government nor some outside, aloof institution designed to pass information to society. It is a social forum which allows society to communicate ideas, which in turn leads to the formation and functioning of self-government. Furthermore, there is no evidence that the press, even prior to the Court's decisions on newsgathering, has ever had any difficulty conducting and reporting its investigations or in accessing the information necessary to criticize the government. Contrary to the pronouncements of the fourth estate model, it is not the investigatory ability of the press that is threatened today; rather, what is at jeopardy today is the opinion-publishing and community "bulletin board" function of the press.

The fourth estate theorists also claim that affirmative rights of newsgathering and investigation are necessary for effective reporting. Effective reporting, however, is an amorphous term. It is very difficult to provide for effective reporting through constitutional law. Rather, effective reporting depends on the many skills that a reporter possesses. Therefore, the quality and scope of journalistic information available to the public depends greatly on the subjective talents of a reporter and not on the particular status of constitutional law.

Advocates of a fourth estate role for the press often claim that the Court should take a functional approach to constitutional claims under the press clause; i.e. whatever functions are essential for a free press should be protected. They then claim that newsgathering is an essential function and should receive appropriate protection. Contrary to that model, however, the revised marketplace model finds that only two protections are vital for a free press: first, a negative liberty protection for the activities of an individual newspaper or press entity; and second, a structure of the press industry which is open and competitive and which allows for public participation in the communications process. Under the first protection, the government cannot intrude upon editorial autonomy or the newsgathering activities of a newspaper; yet the government is not obliged to promote those activities. However, the second constitutional protection provided by the press clause, and discussed below, may require governmental promotion.

C. **The Industry Structure of the Press Necessary to Uphold the Values of a Free Press**

1. **A Competitive Marketplace Allowing Public Participation and the Dissemination of Diverse Opinions.**

For the press to serve its function of providing a forum for communication, for social interaction and for political participation, it must be an industry composed of independent and competitive media outlets. In the newspaper industry, for instance, while each individual newspaper provides a single forum, only several newspapers combined can make up a sufficient social forum or a true marketplace of communication.[453] Multiple forums for expression serve several functions. First, they provide a source of diverse opinions and ideas. Second, they provide different groups in society a natural means of access to the majority-forming political process of a democracy. With multiple and competitive forums, publication of opinions does not hinge upon a single editor's decision.[454] Furthermore, multiple and competitive forums also indicate to the government the degree of acceptance of those ideas. Finally, multiple forums promote citizen involvement and participation in society and government.

The importance of a diverse and competitive press lies not only in the content of ideas expressed but in providing a proper channel for exchange of ideas. Exchange of opinions in a democracy is vital, because it is public opinion which directs society and government. To facilitate this exchange, the press provides both a vital communication link for society and a communication channel between society and government.

A diverse and pluralist society needs an open marketplace to exchange opinions and to allow the attainment of some social consensus among all the individuals and groups in society. Although a single large newspaper may be able to print most of the "hard news" available, it cannot adequately respond to the different opinions of all the different groups in its circulation area. Indeed, there is a recognition that newspapers are not as opinionated today as they were in the past.[455]

Political allegiance of every variety springs from environmental factors, including most importantly the marketplace of ideas.[456] Such a marketplace provides a means by which the various political opinions are expressed in relation to the degree of their acceptance in society. This leads to a more rational and complete process of political action and decision-making. Political groups can then participate in the majority-forming process from the initial grass-roots level. In discussing the nature of a free press, the noted legal scholar, Zechariah Chafee, Jr., stated that "Freedom is not safety but opportunity. Freedom ought to be a means to enable the press to serve the proper functions of communication in a free society."[457]

The communication role played by the press is potentially a two-way street. The public can learn about government actions; and the government by monitoring the contents of the media will be able to gauge public sentiment.[458] Since a democratic government is controlled by the vote, those who govern must be somewhat sensitive to the wishes of the electorate.[459] Thus, although the representative process may be indirect and imperfect, a free press helps bring about the political and social changes desired by the public.

Noting the importance of a competitive press industry, several scholars have read into the First Amendment a guide as to the organization or structure of the overall media industry. For instance, Professor Pool interprets the First Amendment as suggesting that a freely competitive press is the best possible press and that structural reforms may be necessary to achieve such a press. Pool also views the First Amendment as containing some affirmative dimension or some mandate to the government to help the system of freedom of expression work better.[460] Likewise, Professor Emerson asserted that government must affirmatively make available the opportunity for expression as well as protect it from abridgement.[461] Professor Chafee also believed that the First Amendment addressed the quality and effectiveness of our system of public discussion.[462]

Therefore, the idea of the First Amendment carrying a structural dimension is not a novel one. The need for such a dimension has long been seen. The confusion, however, has been in articulating a coherent theory of this structural dimension and in reconciling it with both the speech and press clauses. The revised marketplace model addresses this need. It also rests upon a recognition of the value of structural diversity in the press industry.

Structural diversity in the media will provide the public with a diverse nongovernmentally controlled source of information and perspectives.[463] Such a structurally diverse press industry will naturally check abuses of government and bring to light instances of governmental corruption. Indeed, contrary to the assumptions underlying the fourth estate model, a strong and independent press should be able to function within any information environment.[464] However, structural diversity will not lead to large, powerful and dominating presses, as envisioned by the fourth estate theory.[465] While such institutions may provide a powerful check on government, they will not be an easily accessible source for opinions of the various segments of society.

Structural diversity is also the best way to promote a marketplace for opinion dissemination. Opinion dissemination constituted a primary purpose and function of the press in the eighteenth century.[466] Only lately, coinciding with the rise of the fourth estate model of the press, has investigation taken a priority role over opinion dissemination.[467] Yet though the publication of opinions can always lead to investigation, the prevalence of investigative reporting will not necessarily lead to the airing of a diverse source of opinions.

The free press theories of Professor Pool support the view that a freely competitive press is the best possible press and that structural reforms may be necessary to achieve such a press. Pool identifies two distinct lines of legal precedent: the First Amendment protection of the press and the government regulation of monopolistic common carriers aimed at assuring public access.[468] Recognizing the assumption behind the First Amendment that any writer could gain access to a printing press without the help of government, Pool argues that resource availability ought to determine the degree of regulation of the press.[469] Thus, to the extent that resources for a communications medium are generally scarce or are monopolized, government regulation may be necessary--but only to ensure open access. However, to the extent that a communications medium is decentralized, dispersed and widely available, little or no government regulation is required. Pool argues that regulation is a last recourse, legitimate only if an important communications medium is truly monopolistic.[470] The free press theories of Pool therefore reflect his belief in pluralism and his goal of ensuring that all speakers have maximum opportunity to speak.[471]

Pool even suggests that print publications should be subject to common carrier regulations if monopoly conditions exist.[472] These kind of structural regulations may even be permissible under the Tornillo decision. By holding in Tornillo that the right of access to newspapers violated the First Amendment, the Court prohibited all regulations of media content because those regulations forced the government to intrude into editorial decision making. The Court, however, never discussed structural regulations of print.[473] According to Pool, the First Amendment creates a presumption that entry by news media cannot be blocked. Therefore, government regulations may be in order if media entities enjoy a monopoly status.[474]

In constituting a positive liberty, the press clause may require, as Pool suggests, an affirmative government duty to promote and protect the type of press industry favored by the framers and needed to achieve the values of a free press. Such a concept or duty has received increasing attention among contemporary First Amendment scholars.[475] Though the First

Amendment bars the government from abridging freedom of the press, it does not at all prohibit governmental promotion of First Amendment values in a manner that does not restrain expression. Indeed, blockages often arise in the communications system, and the First Amendment may authorize appropriate remedies. Just as the Constitution empowered the Court in Baker v. Carr to remedy blockages in the political system, the press clause as a positive liberty confers power upon the state to reform the communications system in ways that will promote the constitutional values of a free press.

Lawrence Tribe advocates such an affirmative approach to the First Amendment.[476] Tribe supports the concept that the Amendment contains a positive liberty focus.[477] Recognizing the trend toward concentration and monopolization in the modern media, Tribe finds that:

> "These changes in access to and control over the forms of public communication, and the court's unwillingness to permit regulations that would ameliorate the resulting inequalities in the power to communicate, have eaten away at the average citizen's rights of expression."[478]

Tribe decries the Court's failure to react to the conditions in the press which have prevented the kind of public discussion possible at earlier times in America's history. He notes, for instance, the Court's approval of the Postal Service's practice of banning the placing of unstamped material in mailboxes--a means of communication available to groups without large financial resources--coinciding with its prohibition of limits on individual campaign contributions--a means of communications favoring wealthy groups and individuals.[479] Thus, Tribe would begin to open up the communications marketplace by ending discriminatory governmental restrictions, whether they are explicitly discriminatory or implicitly favor some views and speakers over others.

The revised marketplace model, in viewing the press clause as a positive liberty, envisions an affirmative approach to the press industry. Affirmative ways in which the government might open up the communications marketplace and promote the values of a free press include: economic incentives for small newspapers similar to the reduced postal rates provided by the Rural Newspaper Preservation Act; structural regulations regarding media ownership; the use of "spectrum or user fees" charged to monopolized press entities to subsidize public media outlets; and government incentives to large media corporations to promote diversity or provide services that are unlikely to be currently offered. An interesting request for government power to protect the press occurred when CBS sought the protection of government to fight off corporate takeover attempts. Indeed, given the trend toward increasing corporate concentration in the media industry, the mandate of the press clause may require such changes as reforms in the tax laws which encourage corporate takeovers or which make independent media organizations vulnerable to mergers or acquisitions.

As outlined in the revised marketplace model, the structural diversity of a press industry should be categorized as an "offensive right." Defensive rights, which are those protecting the functions of an individual newspaper, protect against governmental abridgement and interference with a newspaper's operation.[480] Structural diversity of the press as a positive liberty, however, might only be accomplished by offensive rights. Therefore, the public may be able to force government to take affirmative actions to promote structural diversity.[481] To achieve structural diversity in the media, the revised marketplace model suggests such industry reforms as lower entry barriers, so that new and emerging groups can have access to the press and communicate their ideas to society.[482]

The revised marketplace theory of the free press clause incorporates a positive liberty view and seeks to reinvigorate the structure of the modern press so as to better achieve the values served by a free press in a democratic society. It envisions a true communications marketplace ("cafeteria style"), which in turn allows for a diverse source of ideas and a greater opportunity for participation by the public.

The model for the structure of the press industry lies in the constitutional period, when the average citizen not only had access to newspapers but also could set up his or her own printing press. In Tom Paine's time, a variety of viewpoints found outlets through the many penny sheets.[483] Today, however, newspapers are big businesses with high barriers to entry.[484] With ownership concentrated in the newspaper chains, the number of viewpoints printed is limited and the scope of the viewpoints is not representative of the whole society.[485] This lack of structural diversity in the media, as well as high entry barriers, means that new groups and new interests have little access to the press and little ability to communicate their ideas to society. As during the constitutional period, low entry barriers will allow the publication of ideas as those ideas are formed; whereas a mandated right of access as proposed by Jerome Barron would entail a lag time between the formation of those ideas and access of those ideas to the press.

According to the revised marketplace theory, a structurally diverse press serves a valuable role in self-government. This role is achieved by allowing the majority-forming process to be more open and accessible. The theory also holds that the dissemination of diverse opinions holds greater value in a democracy than the power of one newspaper to investigate abuses of government. This view conforms with the Court's decision in Tornillo, which held that government could not force a newspaper to become the marketplace for airing all viewpoints. Under the revised marketplace theory, the marketplace of ideas is produced by a diverse number of competitive newspapers. And unlike the fourth estate model, it does not create a large and monopolistic press industry insensitive to different groups and individuals in society.

2. A Criticism of the Fourth Estate Model of the Press

The "fourth-estate" theory of the press views the First Amendment as protecting the press as an adversarial check on the government. This theory sees the press as an agent of the public, in a separation of powers scheme, that functions to check abuses of governmental power. As an agent of the public, the press constitutes an independent entity with a life and purpose of its own, not just a forum for facilitating communication.[486]

The claim of the press to represent the public can be interpreted in two ways: either the press can purport to act as a professional surrogate for the rights of members of the public as individuals; or the press can purport to act as an unofficial surrogate for the power of the government to represent the public as a whole.[487] The press asserts the first interpretation when it claims to represent the constitutional rights of certain individuals to gather, receive or disseminate information. The press asserts the second interpretation when it claims protection to effectively expose deception in government.

The fourth estate model envisions the press as a direct and independent participant in the political process. In this context, a free press functions to offset the presumed informational advantage that government possesses.[488] And in performing this function, the press takes on its role as a muckraker and as an opponent of the government. It mobilizes different publics than the government represents with respect to a given issue.[489] In this sense, the press serves an equalizing function between government and a disorganized and helpless society.[490]

The press also plays a "governmental" role within the fourth estate model.[491] This role, however, is the limited one of criticizing the three branches of government. The fourth estate model does not recognize the powerful role that the press has in forming political majorities and in providing social cohesion. It does not take a process-view of the press clause and does not see the press as providing open and accessible channels of communication between society and government. Furthermore, though its advocates defend the equalizing function of the fourth estate model, the revised marketplace model more adequately accomplishes such a function by creating a press open to all groups in society.[492] Likewise, those "fourth estatists" who see the press as performing an intermediary function in society--intermediating between government and society--do not recognize that adoption of the marketplace model would also accomplish this function.

There has been much criticism of the fourth estate model of the free press clause. Professor Barron states that it is a mistake to identify the "press" with the "people" and to think that immunity from suit for newspapers is equivalent to enhancing the right of free expression for all members of the community.[493] There is also a problem with viewing the press as an agent of the public. After all, the state is the official representative of the public as it is organized through the process of political participation. The press is at best an unofficial representative of the public as an unorganized group, bound together only by a shared need for information. Indeed, the press is subject to no constraints and has never been elected or chosen by the public to act as its agent. Furthermore, as the ownership of the press becomes concentrated in fewer corporations, the press becomes even less responsive to or representative of the public.

The exclusive focus of the fourth estate model upon the adversarial and watchdog function of the press, though made with the intent to improve the workings of government, actually weakens the democratic foundations of our political system. Throughout American history, the periods of the most aggressive adversarial journalism have also been the periods of greatest public apathy and neglect toward the political process. The muckraking journalism of the late nineteenth and early twentieth centuries provide one such example. Instead of inspiring the public to become politically involved, the muckrakers' ceaseless exposes caused disillusionment and cynicism.[494] The press' harshly adversarial role eroded public trust and alienated the voter from the political process. While the investigatory journalism proved powerful, its mission in allowing citizens to make wiser choices was at odds with its results. Instead, its unintended message to the public was to be suspicious of the political process, to pull back from political commitment, and to stay home on election day.

The political impact of the adversarial muckraking journalism at the turn of the century demonstrates the harm that may occur from an exclusive emphasis on the watchdog functions of a fourth estate press. When the press focuses less on transmitting information and opinions and on achieving an open flow of ideas, and focuses more on acting as an aloof critic and investigator, it can lose touch with the public and eventually diminish public involvement in the process of political communication. This loss of involvement threatens the cohesiveness of society and the operation of the political process.

The health of a democracy depends on public involvement in political activities, i.e., voting, which in turn depends largely on participation in the communicative process. The fourth estate model, however, holds that the health of a democracy depends upon the press' ability to check and expose government. It does not recognize the social values of communication, nor does it answer or even address the problem of voter apathy occurring during periods of exclusive press focus on adversarial journalism. Given this historical logic, adoption of the fourth estate theory would further increase voter apathy. It would also lead to the creation of a bigger, more concentrated and less accountable press. Such a press would provide even fewer and less open communication channels for society, and would weaken the democratic foundation of society.

A recent example of the press taking on an almost exclusive fourth estate role and abandoning a marketplace function occurred during the Vietnam era. Just as with the exposes of the muckrakers, the coverage of Vietnam left much of its audience confused and disillusioned.[495] The press' sole objective of investigatory journalism lifted it outside of the public communication marketplace. It poured out facts to the public, but left the public with little opportunity to process and evaluate those facts through communication of opinions and attitudes. Indeed, the press increasingly read the nation's leadership, rather than the nation's populace, for indications of what was newsworthy and acceptable.[496] Consequently, the public was left with no communication marketplace. The danger, therefore, of a fourth estate function for the press lies in the tendency of an adversarial press to abandon its connection with the public and its role in providing a forum for social communication.

Increasingly, the fourth estate press engages in negative journalism; and negative journalism concentrates on what is wrong with our government and society. Furthermore, an over-emphasis on negative and adversarial reporting has caused a public distrust of the media. Indeed, when the media complained loudly that the Reagan Administration prevented it from covering the Grenada invasion, most Americans sided with the Administration. Many believed that the media would not simply report the invasion, but rather would try to sabotage it.[497] Thus, acting as a fourth estate, the press drills into an increasingly numbed public all the ills of society and government. It provides no outlet or opportunity for the public to reaffirm what is right and valuable. Unsurprisingly, yet contrary to the expectations of media executives, the focus of the press on government scandals has produced feelings of political cynicism and powerlessness.[498]

The fourth estate model effectively enhances and magnifies the power of one of the participants in the communications process--the owners of the mass media--with apparently no thought of imposing on the press concomitant responsibilities to assure that the new protection will actually enlarge and protect opportunities for expression.[499] Furthermore, an adoption of the fourth estate model will only accelerate the trend toward concentration in the media industry. Thus, as American society becomes more diverse and pluralistic, its communication forum will become more concentrated, homogeneous and isolated.

Justice White has been a vocal critic of a fourth estate role for the press.[500] White's view is that the press has enough power and does not need a privileged status. According to White, the real threat is not that of press inhibition, but rather its distortion. He sees the communications industry as powerful and not easily intimidated, and perceives danger in the creation of an imbalance in the communications process.[501] White distinguishes between the concept of the First Amendment as a protective device and the concept of the First Amendment as a creator of a privileged class.[502] According to White, the goals of the monopolized press and the public interest are not always synonymous. Contrary to fourth estate advocates, White believes that First Amendment case law has already given the press vast special protection.[503] However, an important aspect of the fourth estate model is that it does not give special protection to an institution, but simply gives added powers to particular newspapers--those newspapers that exist in our monopolistic industry.

According to the fourth estate model, the press must have power as a separate institution to serve as an independent check on the government, and therefore must be guaranteed effective means to gather the news. However, under this model the press publishes what it gathers itself, rather than publishing the ideas that come to it through an interacting society. The fourth estate model primarily focuses upon the public as an audience rather than participant in the communication process. It favors the interests of the audience to hear over the individual's interest or opportunity in participating in public discussions.

In essence, the fourth estate theory creates a fourth bureaucracy with substantial power and quite separate from the general public. The press then becomes much more than conduits of the news, and no longer serves as middlemen between the events and the public. In fact, as a fourth estate the press achieves such power in itself that it becomes the focus of the news. Indeed, over the last several decades, the power and practices of the news media have become a substantial part of the news. Yet, given the fact that the news media has become the news, the failure to cover the increasing concentration of media ownership and its effects on democratic society casts doubt upon the press' watchdog abilities.[504]

CHAPTER VI

CONCLUSION

The revised marketplace model of the First Amendment best serves the values of a free press in a democratic society. The model has a two-part effect. First, it affords defensive protection to each individual media outlet for the performance of that individual entity's press and speech functions. This can be analogized to a negative liberty, and is similar to Justice White's view of the press clause--whereby a newspaper is given protective status to carry out its functions, but is not afforded any special affirmative rights. The second part of the model focuses on the structure of the industry. Unlike the fourth estate model, however, it does not create an independent entity to perform certain "governmental" functions. Instead, the model looks at the physical make-up of the communications "marketplace" and tries to achieve diversity of expression and wide public participation in the social and political communication process.

According to the revised marketplace model, the press provides a link between society and government and serves as a channel of communications. Such a communications channel encourages diverse sources of opinions and allows active citizen participation in the majority-forming processes of a democracy. Unlike the aim of the fourth estate model, the press does not represent the public or act as an agent of society in its dealings with government. Rather, the press acts as a channel for communications passing through society and from society to government. Thus, a more natural interaction can take place between society and government. The revised marketplace model puts high emphasis on citizen participation, on the idea that there must be natural communication among society in order for government to develop from that, and also on the importance of opinions as compared with investigative facts.

There has been much criticism in recent years of the marketplace metaphor. However, the marketplace metaphor being criticized is the one espoused by Justice Holmes. That marketplace metaphor did not describe how a press should be organized and did not adopt the values articulated in the revised marketplace model. Instead, it only looked at the social benefits or side effects that occurred from a free press--the attainment of truth from a marketplace of ideas. Thus, the marketplace metaphor served as a justification rather than as a true model of the press. It is now quite easy to criticize this marketplace model since a true marketplace has long ceased to exist, due to the increased concentration of ownership in the media industry.[505]

Professor Barron has criticized the marketplace of ideas metaphor, arguing that it provides a romantic view of the First Amendment and that currently there is an inadequate "right of access" of the public to the media. Barron also argues that the marketplace metaphor did not adequately address all the nongovernmental obstructions to free expression.[506] Finally, Barron states that changes in the communications industry itself have destroyed any equilibrium in the marketplace.[507] According to Barron:

> A realistic view of the First Amendment requires recognition that a right of expression is somewhat thin if it can be exercised only at the sufferance of the managers of mass communications . . . . Too little attention has been given to defining the purposes which the First Amendment protection is designed to achieve and to identifying the addressees of that protection.[508]

The revised marketplace model, however, conceives of a different marketplace model than the one criticized by Professor Barron.

Professor Benno Schmidt has likewise criticized the marketplace metaphor, again citing the current problem of media concentration.[509] He is also critical of the utilitarian model of First Amendment analysis represented in the marketplace of ideas metaphor and suggests that the metaphor looks exclusively at what system will produce the most diverse speech.[510] Schmidt's theory views the marketplace metaphor, as do most critics, as only directed to the provision of diverse speech. The revised marketplace model, however, espouses many other values--i.e., citizen participation in the majority-forming process, and the building of democratic society.

Advocates of the fourth estate model of the press criticize the marketplace model on the ground that it prevents the development of a strong press that would take positions on public issues. As one fourth estate advocate argues:

> The marketplace conception is antithetical to the press' function of taking positions on matters of public interest . . . [S]afeguarding this function of the press as an adversarial

monitor of the government is more important than inquiring whether the coverage is balanced or partisan, responsible or irresponsible.[511]

Yet, contrary to this argument, the marketplace conception is not antithetical to the press' function of taking positions on matters of public interest. Indeed, the press does not have to take positions on matters of public interest. It is the public that takes such positions and communicates those ideas through the press. If there is structural diversity in the press, matters of public interest will be communicated through the press.

The overriding criticism of the marketplace metaphor, however, lies in the present day reality in the media industry. The drafters never had reason to anticipate a marketplace of ideas dominated by a few in command of the mass media.[512] Yet the economics of the communications industry has concentrated the ability to participate effectively in public debate into a substantially smaller circle of persons.[513] It is this problem that the revised marketplace theory addresses.

The current state of the monopolized media has caused a great public uproar and backlash, including a flood of libel suits. Critics of the media argue that concentration in the media entails a reduction in the diversity of views disseminated to the public.[514] Yet the problem with adopting this criticism as the only justification of a marketplace metaphor is that currently we might be getting all the speech we need. However, that speech is not the result of a wide degree of public participation. The revised marketplace theory attempts to meet both these goals.

The revised marketplace model interprets the press clause in light of the great debate in both the courts and among legal scholars about the meaning and nature of the press clause. As with all constitutional questions, the first focus of analysis is into the historical evidence to try to determine the intent of the framers. An historical examination into the actual conditions of the colonial and revolutionary press shows that it was an open and competitive industry and played an important political role. In short, the press acted as a forum for political debate. The colonists used the newspapers to convey their political ideas to the rest of society. The press was also a vital tool in unifying society in the political struggle against Britain. The early press did not act as an independent entity; instead, it was a channel of communication for colonial society.

At first glance, the press clause literally seems to protect a physical entity--the press. That language, along with the historical conditions of the press, indicates that the framers of the First Amendment protects the press as a competitive industry within society. The revised marketplace model argues that the press clause must be viewed as protecting a different freedom from that protected by the speech clause. Whereas the speech clause protects individual rights, the press clause serves mainly to ensure the protection of a particular type of press industry. This is a type of industry that existed at the time of framing of the First Amendment--an open, competitive and easily accessible press.

The revised marketplace model is supported not only by the historical evidence surrounding the framers' experience with a free press, but also by the values of a free press in a democratic society. Given these values and given the functions that we expect of a free press, it is argued that the revised marketplace model should be used to interpret the press clause. Under the revised marketplace model, values such as citizen participation, political opinion, and open channels of communication are more important than simply the legal power of the press to investigate certain aspects of governmental workings.

The revised marketplace theory of the press clause stands in direct opposition to the fourth estate theory as proposed by Justice Stewart and currently in great popularity among First Amendment scholars. Indeed, the fourth estate model is based perhaps more upon reactions to recent history in which the press has opposed an apparently secretive and corrupt government--i.e., Watergate and Vietnam--than upon an overall analysis into the historical workings of the press and the values expected of a free press in a democratic society.

Nearly a century ago, Lord Bryce in The American Commonwealth dissected the functions of newspapers into three categories: narrator, advocate and weather vane. The fourth estate model, however, ignores all but one function. It especially ignores the opinion role historically served by the press. As mirrors of public opinion, newspapers when lumped together have given expression to nearly every view and have greatly increased the number of persons contributing ideas to the communications marketplace. Yet in elevating investigative reporting above all other press functions, the fourth estate model ignores these vital functions and roles performed by the press throughout history. The revised marketplace model seeks to revive the historical values and purposes of a free press as articulated by Lord Bryce.

ENDNOTES

1. Thomas I. Emerson, *The System of Freedom of Expression* (New York: Random House, 1970), 15.

2. For a general discussion of media concentration and decline in competition in the newspaper industry, see *Iowa Law Review* 60.

3. Not until 1965 was an act of Congress held invalid by the Supreme Court on grounds that it violated the First Amendment. *Lamont v. Postmaster General*, 381 U.S. 301 (1965).

4. For critical surveys of the First Amendment decisions of the Burger Court see Archibald Cox, "Foreward: Freedom of Expression in the Burger Court," *Harvard Law Review* 94 (1980): 1; Thomas I. Emerson, "First Amendment Doctrine and the Burger Court," *California Law Review* 68 (1980): 422.

5. See Cox, "Freedom of Expression in the Burger Court," 72 n. 3 ("The most striking aspect of the work of the Burger Court has been the insistence of the Justices upon presenting individual views . . . "). See also Emerson, "First Amendment Doctrine," 423-40 n. 3 (summarizing particular instances of scholarly agreement and dispute with respect to underlying values).

6. Ithiel DeSola Pool, *Technologies of Freedom* (Cambridge: Harvard University Press, 1983), has outlined the different models for different types of communications. Thus, according to Pool, the First Amendment has been interpreted in different ways for different technologies; i.e., radio, television, cable television, and print media.

7. Pool describes the first model--the no regulation model--on pages 55-74; analyzes the second model--the common carrier model--on pages 75-107; and discusses the third model--the regulatory model--on pages 116-35.

8. See *Houchins v. KQED, Inc.*, 438 U.S. 1 (1978); *Zurcher v. Stanford Daily*, 436 U.S. 547 (1978); *Bell v. Procunier*, 417 U.S. 817 (1974); and *Branzburg v. Hayes*, 408 U.S. 665 (1972).

9. David Anderson, "The Origins of the Press Clause," UCLA Law Review 30 (1983): 459.

10. The press has lost numerous Supreme Court cases in which it claimed some right not available to everyone under the speech clause. See Herbert v. Lando, 441 U.S. 153, 160 (1979) (exemption from discovery of journalists' thought processes); Houchins v. KQED, Inc., 438 U.S. 1, 8-9 (1978) (-(access to jail); Zurcher v. Stanford Daily, 436 U.S. 547, 563-67 (1978) (exemption from police search); Nixon v. Warner Communications, Inc., 435 U.S. 589, 608-10 (1978) (access to Watergate tapes); Saxbe v. Washington Post Co., 417 U.S. 843, 850 (1974) (access to prisons); Pell v. Procunier, 417 U.S. 817, 834 (1974) (access to prisons); Pittsburgh Press Co. v. Pittsburgh Common on Human Relations, 413 U.S. 376, 381-83 (1973) (exemption from antidiscrimination regulations); Branzburg v. Hayes, 408 U.S. 665, 684-86 (1972) (refusal to disclose confidential sources); Associated Press v. United States, 326 U.S. 1, 19-20 (1945) (exemption from antitrust laws).

11. Two of our most prominent First Amendment theorists, Chafee and Emerson, warn us that the historical inquiry is futile, either because "the framers had no very clear idea as to what they meant" (see Zechariah Chafee, review of Free Speech and its Relation to Self-Government, by Alexander Meiklejohn, Harvard Law Review 62 [1949]: 898), or because it is impossible at this late date to ascertain what they meant (see T. Emerson, "Colonial Intentions and Current Realities of the First Amendment," University of Pennsylvania Law Review 125 [1977]: 737). Our most prominent First Amendment historian, Leonard Levy, believes it is possible to ascertain what the framers mean (to wit, very little) but tells us it does not matter: that we are not bound by their understanding anyway. L. Levy, Legacy of Suppression: Freedom of Speech and Press in Early American History (Cambridge: Harvard University Press, 1960), 4.

Nimmer asserted that "[h]istory casts little light on the question here posed . . . . But as we have seen in other constitutional contexts, the original understanding of the Founders is not necessarily controlling." Nimmer, "Is Freedom of the Press a Redundancy," 640. Lange briefly examined the eighteenth-century literature on press freedom and found the evidence for Stewart's view "not entirely persuasive." He noted that neither the fourth estate metaphor nor the press as we know it had yet been conceived when the First Amendment was drafted. Lange, "Speech and Press Clauses," 90.

12. In Near v. Minnesota, 283 U.S. 697 (1931) and Nebraska Press Association v. Stuart, 423 U.S. 1011 (1975), prohibitions against publication fell because of the heavy presumption against

prior restraints--a presumption that also attaches when government attempts to restrain nonmedia speakers. The "actual malice" rule of <u>New York Times Co. v. Sullivan</u>, 376 U.S. 254 (1964), apparently was not derived exclusively from the press clause because it protected the four nonmedia defendants in that case as well as the <u>Times</u> and has since been applied in cases in which there was no media defendant at all. In the contempt context, even before the Supreme Court invoked the press clause to protect editors who dared to criticize the judiciary, it extended such protection to Harry Bridges, the longshoremen's leader.

At the time these cases were decided, the existence of the press clause may have been crucial. In <u>Near</u>, for example, the Supreme Court came within one vote of sustaining a prior restraint. Absent the press clause, with its undisputed historical objective of prohibiting prior restraints, the decision might have gone the other way. Once these "press" cases had been decided, however, the Court invariably held that the same rights were available to everyone under the speech clause.

13. Justice Douglas, however, did accord the press clause independent significance: "The press has a preferred position in our constitutional scheme, not to enable it to make money, not to set newsmen apart as a favored class, but to bring fulfillment to the public's right to know." <u>Branzburg v. Hayes</u>, 408 U.S. 665, 721 (1972) (Douglas, J., dissenting). See also <u>Saxbe v. Washington Post Co.</u>, 417 U.S. 843, 863 (1974) (Powell, J., dissenting).

Chief Justice Burger is the only member of the Court who has expressed hostility toward the prospect of specific constitutional protection for the press, and even he concedes that the question is still open. See <u>First Nat'l Bank v. Bellotti</u>, 435 U.S. 765, 796802 (1978) (Burger, C. J., concurring). Burger argues that the press clause should not be read to give the institutional press any freedoms not enjoyed by all others, because first, "the history of the Clause does not suggest that the authors contemplated a 'special' or 'institutional' privilege,, (798), and second, the task of defining "the press" would involve some governmental entity in a process "reminiscent of the abhorred licensing system of Tudor and Stuart England--a system the First Amendment was intended to ban from this country" (801).

14. In <u>Pell v. Procunier</u>, 94 S. Ct. 2800, 2827 (1974), and <u>Saxbe v. Washington Post Co.</u>, 94 S. Ct. 2811, 2827 (1974), the Court, borrowing from its opinion in the reporter privilege case, <u>Branzburg v. Hayes</u>, 408 U.S. 665, 707 (1972), acknowledged that "newsgathering is not without its First Amendment protections . . . for without some protection for seeking out the news, freedom of the press could be eviscerated.11 94 S. Ct. at 2809. The concession that the freedom of the press clause protected a right not

available under the freedom of speech clause was quickly withdrawn, however, by the further comment that "the Constitution does not, however, require government to accord the press special access to information not shared by members of the public generally." 94 S. Ct. at 2810.

15. Scholarly commentators have frequently advocated an institutional interpretation. See Randall Bezanson, "The New Free Press Guarantee," Virginia Law Review 63 (1977): 731; Margaret Blanchard, "The Institutional Press and its First Amendment Privileges," Supreme Court Review, (1978): 225; Victor Blasi, "The Checking Value in First Amendment Theory," American Bar Foundation Research Journal, (1977): 523; Melville Nimmer, "Is Freedom of the Press a Redundancy: What Does it Add to Freedom of Speech," Hastings Law Journal 261 (1975): 639; J. Potter Stewart, "Or of the Press," Hastings Law Journal 26 (1975): 631. For contrary analysis taking the position that definitional and functional problems prevent separation of speech and press see David Lange, "The Speech and Press Clauses," UCLA Law Review 23 (1975): 77; William VanAlstyne, "The Hazards to the Press of Claiming a Preferred Position," Hastings Law Journal 28 (1977): 761.

16. Stewart, "Or of the Press."

17. Ibid., 634.

18. William Van Alystyne, "The First Amendment and the Free Press," Hofstra Law Review 9 (1980): 1.

19. Nimmer, "Is Freedom of the Press a Redundancy."

20. See Nicholas Johnson and James M. Hoak Jr., "Media Concentration: Some Observations on the United States' Experience," Iowa Law Review 56 (1970): 267.

21. In Miami Harold Publishing Company v. Tornillo, 418 U.S. 241, 249 (1974), the Court acknowledged the adverse implications of concentrated media ownership. This Court also specifically noted the declining number of newspapers, the development of newspaper chains, national newspapers, and wire services, the prevalence of single newspaper cities, and the elimination of competition among various media within a geographic area.

Former President Carter recently drew attention to the dilemma posed by this concentration of the ability to communicate with a significant segment of the public. In responding to false allegations made by the only remaining daily newspaper in Washington that Carter bugged Blair House while it was occupied by president-elect Reagan, Carter observed that unlike himself, the great majority of Americans lack sufficient access to the press to correct falsehoods that it spreads. Washington Post, 25 October 1981, p. 7, col. 2.

22. "Centralization of communications and denial of access to the media isolate the individual and discourage his responsible participation in public affairs." Roscoe Barrow, "The Fairness Doctrine: A Double Standard for Electronic and Print Media," Hastings Law Journal 26 (1975): 661.

23. TIME, 21 November 1983, 55.

24. This discussion of the black press taken from Patrick S. Washburn, A Question of Sedition: The Federal Government's Investigation of the Black Press During World War II (N.Y. 1986).

25. In stressing the importance of competitive media, the courts have been especially vigilant in enforcing the antitrust laws when dealing with the structure and practices of the communication industries. The Supreme Court of 1953 stated that "A vigorous and dauntless press is a chief source feeding the flow of democratic expression and controversy which maintains the institutions of a free society." Times-Picayune Publishing Company v. United States, 345 U.S. 594, 602 (1953). The Court of Appeals for the District of Columbia has placed an affirmative duty on the FCC to encourage competition. In Joseph v. F. C. C., 404 F.2d 207, 211 (D. C. Cir., 1968), the court said that "The public welfare requires the Commission to provide the widest possible dissemination of information from diverse and antagonistic sources and to guard against undue concentration of control of the communications power." See also Scripps-Howard Radio, Inc. v. F. C. C., 189 F.2d 677, 683 (D. C. Cir., 1951). In a more recent decision, Judge Tamm, after discussing the necessity of free and competitive media, went on to write that "It is also becoming increasingly obvious that application of antitrust doctrines in regulating the mass media is not solely a question of sound economic policy; it is also an important means of achieving the goals posited by the First Amendment." Alhale v. F. C. C., 625F.2d 556, 561 (D. C. Cir., 1970) (concurring opinion). As Judge Tamm wrote, a democracy will have failed if ever the people "feel that they are being cheated out of the vigorous marketplace of ideas promised by the First Amendment" (566).

26. In Technologies of Freedom, Professor Pool outlines the history underlying the regulation of the broadcast media by the FCC.

27. See United States v. Associated Press, 326 U.S. 1 (1945).

28. Georgetown Law Journal 60 (1972): 1006.

29. Pool, Technologies of Freedom, 106.

30. For a discussion of the economic history of the print media and its relevance to the First Amendment, see Bruce Owen, Economics and Freedom of Expression: Media Structure and the First Amendment (Cambridge, Mass.: Ballinger Publishing Company, 1975), 33-85.

31. One aspect of the media's role is its importance in the marketplace of ideas. See Red Lyon Broadcasting Company v. F. C. C., 395 U.S. 367, 377 (1969); New York Times Company v. Sullivan, 376 U.S. 254, 269 (1964).

32. Jerome Barron, "Access to the Press--A New First Amendment Right," Harvard Law Review 80 (1967): 1641.

33. Ibid.

34. Benno C. Schmidt, Jr., Freedom of the Press V. Public Access (New York: Praeger Publishers, 1976), 33.

35. U.S. v. Abrams, 250 U.S. 616 (1919). For insight into the views of Holmes, see Gerald Gunther, "Learned Hand and the Origins of Modern First Amendment Doctrine," Stanford Law Review 27 (1975): 719.

36. In Freedom of the Press, Schmidt perceives that the marketplace of ideas metaphor may be used as a sword for government intrusion. Its risks arise from its emphasis on the value of efficiency. The danger in thinking about First Amendment problems in that way alone may lead us to shortchange ourselves by forgetting what is essential to our integrity as a people and by trying to maximize the amount of speech in the system. See L. C.

Bollinger, review of <u>Freedom of the Press v. Public Access</u>, by Benno Schmidt, <u>Columbia Law Review</u> 76 (1976): 1361.

37. Stewart, "Or of the Press," 634.

38. Francis Fisher, "Free Speech and High Tech," <u>Michigan Law Review</u> 82 (February 1984): 983.

39. See Nimmer, "Is Freedom of the Press a Redundancy," 648. "History casts little light on the question here posed. . . . Nothing in the fragmentary records of debate attending the adoption of the First Amendment suggests that the founding fathers had . . . any distinction [between the freedom of speech and freedom of press clauses) in mind, when they chose to protect both freedom of speech and of the press against abridgement." See also, Martin Rooney, "Freedom of the Press," 34. "One certainty emerges from a review of the history of both the speech and press clauses: the true intent of the First Amendment's authors is essentially unknown."

40. See Pool, <u>Technologies of Freedom</u>. Professor Barrow argues against the double standard on the following grounds: First, the Supreme Court has refused to equate the economic limitation on the number of daily newspapers with the natural limitation of broadcasting; second, the Supreme Court has refused to extend to the print media the concept used in its broadcasting decisions that viewers and listeners hold the paramount position in the accommodations of the various First Amendment interests; and third, the Supreme Court gives no weight to the interest of readers of a newspaper in being informed, rather than misinformed, on public issues. Barrow, "The Fairness Doctrine," 706.

41. John Lofton, <u>The Press as Guardian of the First Amendment</u> (Charleston: University of South Carolina Press, 1980).

42. E. Emery, <u>The Press and America</u> (Englewood Cliffs, N.J. Prentiss Hall, 1962) 126-27.

43. Levy, <u>Legacy of Suppression</u>, 126-27 ("The colonists gave little independent thought and even less expression to a theory of unfettered debate . . . ").

44. Lofton, <u>The Press as Guardian</u>, 4.

45. On 9 November 1775 the Continental Congress adopted a secrecy resolution providing that any member who violated the agreement by divulging any part of the proceedings without consent was to be expelled from Congress and "deemed an enemy to the liberties of America." See Charles C. Tansill, ed., Documents Illustrative of the Formation of the Union of American States, (New Rochelle, N.Y.: Arlington House, 1972), 18. There was no very pointed objection from the press, and the most important convention in American history went largely unreported. See Frank L. Mott, American Journalism, a History, 3d ed. (New York: Macmillan Co., 1962), n. 259, 119.

46. Ibid.

47. Lofton, The Press as Guardian, 6.

48. According to the patriots, liberty of speech was the right of those who spoke the speech of liberty. Tory editors were subjected to harassment. See Leonard Levy, Freedom of Speech and Press in Early American History, (New York: Harper & Row, 1963), 64, 69, 176, 183; and Leonard Levy, Jefferson and Civil Liberties, (Cambridge, Mass.: Belknap Press, 1963), 12.

49. Levy, Legacy of Suppression, 126.

50. Professor Emerson, a leading constitutional scholar, has observed that it is "by no means clear exactly what the colonists had in mind, or just what they expected from the guaranty of freedom of speech, press, assembly and petition." Emerson, "Colonial Intentions," 737. Another scholar has noted that the precise motives of those who drafted the press clause "are unlikely to be discovered now, if indeed they ever were ascertainable." Anthony A. Lewis, "Preferred Position for Journalism," Hofstra Law Review 7 (1979): 599. See also Zechariah Chafee, Free Speech in the United States (New York: Atheneum, 1941) 3-35; Bertrand Hudson, Freedom of Speech and Press in America, (Cambridge: Harvard University Press, 1963); and Henry Drinker, Some Observations on the Four Freedoms of the First Amendment, (Boston: Boston University Press, 1957), 2-6.

51. "The Speech and Press Clause of the First Amendment as Ordinary Language," Harvard Law Review 87 (1973): 392-93.

52. Charles Marshall, "Examining the Institutional Interpretation of the Press Clause," Texas Law Review 58 (1979): 176.

53. See note 20.

54. Levy, Legacy of Suppression, 215. Neither the great Bill of Rights advocates such as Jefferson, Patrick Henry, Richard Henry Lee, and George Mason, nor the newspapers, pamphlets, or the ratifying convention debates provide insight.

55. Professor Levy notes that:

> It is astonishing to discover that the debate on the Bill of Rights, during the ratification controversy, was conducted at a level of abstraction so vague as to convey the impression that Americans of 1787 to 1788 had only the most nebulous conception of the meaning of the particular rights they sought to ensure; indeed many of the principal advocates of a Bill of Rights had only a nebulous idea of what it ought to contain. Freedom of the press was everywhere a grand topic for declamation, but the insistent demand for its protection on parchment was not accompanied by a reasoned analysis of what it meant, how far it extended, and under what circumstances it might be limited.

Levy, Legacy of Suppression, 214-15.

56. Levy states as follows:

> "But the history of the ratification indicates no passion on the part of anyone to grind underfoot the common law of liberty of the press. Indeed, the history of the framing and ratification of the First Amendment and the other nine scarcely manifests a passion on the part of anyone connected with the process. Considering its immediate background, our precious Bill of Rights was in the main the chance result of certain federalists, having been reluctantly forced to capitalize for their own cause the propaganda that had been originated in vain by the anti-federalists for ulterior purposes. Thus, the party that had first opposed the Bill of Rights inadvertently wound up with the responsibility for its framing and ratification, while the party that had at first professedly wanted it discovered too

late that its framing and ratification were not only embarrassing but inexpedient.

Levy, Legacy of Suppression, 233.

Another author states that the Bill of Rights, including the First Amendment, was ultimately adopted not because of a universal belief in its necessity nor because of adherence to a defined theory of free expression but as a compromise in the struggle between antifederalists who opposed the new Constitution and the federalists who supported the Constitution. Lofton, The Press as Guardian, 11.

57. Levy, Legacy of Suppression, 236.

58. Besides Levy, see Edward Corwin, "Freedom of Speech and Press Under the First Amendment," Yale Law Journal 30 (1920): 48.

59. "Media and the First Amendment in a Free Society," Georgetown Law Journal 60 (1972): 876.

60. Chafee, review of Free Speech and its Relation to Self-Government, by Alexander Meiklejohn.

61. Levy, Legacy of Suppression, 236.

62. Ibid.

63. 103 S. Ct. 1365, 1372 n. 6.

64. The commission was chaired by Robert M. Hutchins.

65. Levy, Emergence of a Free Press, 272.

66. Robert, Brest, "The Misconceived Quest for the Original Understanding," Boston University Law Review, 60 (1980): 204; F. Schauer, "An Essay on Constitutional Language," UCLA Law Review, 29 (1982): 804-12.

67. Mott, American Journalism, 46.

68. For a detailed description of printing processes of the colonial presses, see August Klapper, The Printer in Eighteenth Century Williamsburg, ed. Parke Rowse and M. W. Thomas, Williamsburg Craft Series No. 1 (1955), 15-21.

69. Schlesinger, Prelude to Independence, 60.

70. In effect, the colonial editor performed all the functions of publishing a newspaper. Schlesinger, Prelude to Independence, 60-61.

71. Steven Botein, "Printers and the American Revolution," in The Press and the American Revolution, ed. Bernard Bailyn and John B. Hench (Worcester: American Antiquarian Society, 1980), 16.

72. Even the successful newspapers had difficulty in getting paid by subscribers. James Parker of the New York Gazette or Weekly Post Boy declared that "in the best of my times, at least a quarter failed to pay." His colleague on the New York Weekly Journal complained that some of his subscribers were in arrears for "upwards of seven years." According to the owners of the Connecticut Journal, "they have not for this year past received from all the customers for this journal so much money as they have expended for the blank paper on which it is printed." Beverly McAnear, "James Parker v. New York Province," New York History, XXII (1941): 7, quoting Parker in 1759; New York Weekly Journal, 18 March 1751; Connecticut Journal, 2 April 1113.

73. Botein, "Printers," 17. The best account of the American trade is still Lawrence C. Roth, The Colonial Printer, 2d ed. (Portland, Maine: 1938). On diversity of enterprise see especially chapter 9. It was not unusual to find a general store attached to the printing house as well as a bookstore. Botein, "Printers," 17.

74. Arthur M. Schlesinger, Prelude to Independence (New York: Alfred A. Knopf, 1958), 53. See also Botein, "Printers," 17. Thus, the editor was primarily an entrepreneur who had other affairs besides the publishing and printing of a newspaper. He was also a job printer and the local postmaster as well as the public printer. Mott, American Journalism, 59.

75. Schlesinger, Prelude to Independence, 53.

76. <u>Pennsylvania Gazette</u>, 11 December 1740. Franklin's elevation to the office of Deputy Postmaster General in 1753 gave him dominion over almost the entire American service, and Franklin's peremptory dismissal from this station twenty-one years later was to furnish the colonists with a fresh grievance against the ministry. Schlesinger, <u>Prelude to Independence</u>, 53.

77. See Robert M. Weir "The Role of the Newspaper Press in the Southern Colonies on the Eve of the Revolution: An Interpretation," in <u>The Press and the American Revolution</u>, ed. Bernard Bailyn and John B. Hench (Worcester: American Antiquarian Society, 1980), 99.

78. See Weir, "Role of the Newspaper Press," 108-11.

79. Solomon Lutnick, <u>The American Revolution and the British Press, 1775-1783</u> (Columbia, Mo.: University of Missouri Press, 1967), appendix; Steven Botein, "Mere Mechanics and an Open Press: The Business and Political Strategies of Colonial American Printers," <u>Perspectives in American History</u> 9 (1975): 143.

80. See Weir, "Role of the Newspaper Press," 110-11.

81. Ibid., 111.

82. Roth, <u>The Colonial Printer</u>, chapter 9. Those who sought a printer's skills, news, or goods were predominantly men of property. Thus, the paying customers usually came from the upper levels of society. Only where a printer's competitive position was exceptionally strong or local leaders were unusually divided could he afford to alienate a substantial portion of them. Weir, "Role of the Newspaper Press," 113-14.

83. Isiah Thomas neatly summed up the problem in a capsule memoir of Franklin's nephew, Benjamin Mecom:

> He was handsomely dressed, wore a powdered bob wig, ruffles and gloves; gentlemen like appendages which the printers of that day did not assume--and, thus appareled, would often assist, for an hour, at the press.

Isiah Thomas, <u>The History of Printing in America</u>, Vol. 1 (New York: Weathervane Books, 1874), 351.

84. Mott, American Journalism, 46.

85. Botein, "Printers," 18.

86. As often in the English provinces but not in London, a printer in America might face no competition but still have few clients because local demand for his product was apt to be slight. See Geoffrey Allen Cranfield, The Development of the Provincial Newspaper, 1700 to 1760 (Cambridge: Oxford University Press, 1962), 118.

87. Schlesinger, Prelude to Independence, 54.

88. For a discussion of newspaper circulations during the colonial period, see Schlesinger, Prelude to Independence, appendix A, 303-04.

89. For a discussion on the content of colonial newspapers, see Weir, "Role of the Newspaper Press," 117-19.

90. Donald H. Stewart, The Opposition Press of the Federalist Period (Albany: State University of New York Press, 1969), 4.

91. William Chenery, Freedom of the Press (New York: Harcourt Brace, 1955), 144.

92. Stewart, Opposition Press, 20.

93. Ibid., 60.

94. Emery, The Press and America, 68.

95. Weir, "Role of the Newspaper Press," 132.

96. Stewart, Opposition Press, 4.

97. Weir, "Role of the Newspaper Press," 132.

98. Schlesinger, *Prelude to Independence*, 61.

99. Weir, "Role of the Newspaper Press," 134. See also Richard L. Merritt, "Public Opinion in Colonial America: Content Analyzing the Colonial Press," *Public Opinion Quarterly* 27 (1963): 363; Cranfield, *Development of the Provincial Newspaper*, 259.

100. Weir, "Role of the Newspaper Press," 136.

101. Ibid., 137.

102. See Cranfield, *Development of the Provincial Newspaper*, 118; Botein, "Printers," 19. The literature on liberty of expression in the colonies is vast but mainly tangential to the point here, since most of what has been written does not take into account the perspectives of printers. A useful overview of some general issues raised by the secondary literature may be found in Leonard Levy's preface to the paperback edition of *Legacy of Suppression*, published as *Freedom of Speech and Press in Early American History; Legacy of Suppression* (Cambridge: Harvard University Press, 1963).

103. Merrill Jensen, *The New Nation: A History of the U. S. During the Confederation*, (New York: Knopf, 1 50), 430.

104. *Pennsylvania Gazette*, 10 June 1731.

105. Botein, "Printers," 20.

106. *Pennsylvania Gazette*, 10 June 1731.

107. Botein, "Printers," 21.

108. Sidney Kobre, *The Development of the Colonial Newspaper* (Pittsburgh: Colonial Press, Inc., 1944), 147-48, lists thirty-nine newspapers as patriot and eighteen as Tory.

109. Botein, "Printers, " 32.

110. Phillip Davidson, *Propaganda and the American Revolution, 1763 to 1783* (Chapel Hill, N. C.: University of North Carolina Press, 1941), 304-07; Thomas, *History of Printing*, vol. II, 333-34.

111. Anderson, "The Origins of the Press Clause, " 466.

112. Thomas, *History of Printing*, vol. 1, 347-48; O. M. Dickerson, "British Control of American Newspapers on the Eve of the Revolution," *New England Quarterly* 24 (1951): 455-59.

113. Botein, "Printers," 39.

114. Ibid., 37-40.

115. Catherine Snell Crary, "The Tory and the Spy: The Double Life of James Rivington," *William and Mary Quarterly* 16 (1959): 61-72; Richard F. Hixson, *Isaac Collins: A Quaker Printer in Eighteenth Century America* (New Brunswick, N. J.: Rutgers University Press, 1968), 97-98.

116. The patriot cause after all was generally popular and hence likely to be profitable as well. Schlesinger, *Prelude to Independence*, 137, 165; Davidson, *Propaganda*, 304. Although it is unclear whether or to what extent purely political printing grew to become a significant business of its own during the revolutionary years, it is obvious that the political loyalties of printers could be crucial in determining who would be their customers or readers. See Peter J. Parker, "The Philadelphia Printer: A Study of an Eighteenth Century Businessman," *Business History Review* 40 (1966): 38.

117. See *New York Journal*, 5 January 1775, *Pennsylvania Journal*, 17 August 1774.

118. See "A Real Churchman," appearing in the *New York Gazeteer*, 9 January 1775.

119. Botein, "Printers, " 49.

120. On the development of partisan journalism after the Revolutionary War, see, generally, Stewart, *Opposition Press*.

121. Quoted in Thomas, <u>History of Printing</u>, vol. 2, 403.

122. Owen, <u>Economics and Freedom of Expression</u>, 6.

123. Ibid., 41. This type of entry, however, never occurred during the colonial period except in the regular course of a printer's printing career which began at an early age.

124. Ibid., 41. Owen found only one example of entry by a nonprinter by means of acquiring a printing establishment for the purpose of publishing his own views.

125. According to Owen, the most famous example of this third type of entry--entry by influence--was the publication of the <u>New York Weekly Journal</u> by John Peter Zenger.

126. One cause of this change is seen by many scholars as the press's role in opposing the Stamp Act of 1765. Owen, <u>Economics and Freedom of Expression</u>, 42. Also, see later section in this paper on the Stamp Act.

127. These statistics are taken from Owen, <u>Economics and Freedom of Expression</u>, 64.

128. Owen states that this rapid increase in the number of newspapers can be explained by improved printing technology, better conditions in the paper industry, and changes in the demand for newspapers. Ibid., 43-44.

129. Ibid.

130. Ibid., 43. Owen cites this as evidence of his assertion that the press industry was characterized by small-scale, competitive presses.

131. Botein, "Printers," 21, 33, 44, 45.

132. Schlesinger, <u>Prelude to Independence</u>, 216.

133. Mott, *American Journalism*, 113-14.

134. Mott, *American Journalism*, 113-14.

135. Owen finds that the newspaper publisher during the revolutionary period still behaved as a conduit for news and opinions; however, the overwhelming majority of newspapers at that time began to identify strongly with one political group or another. Owen, *Economics and Freedom of Expression*, 44.

136. See Cheney, *Freedom of the Press*, 143-45; Mott, *American Journalism*, 113-14.

137. Lofton, *The Press as Guardian*, 11.

138. Lofton identifies one cause of this as being such highly political events as the French Revolution and Jay's Treaty, which furthered the development of political parties, with newspapers serving as vehicles for those increasingly vehement partisan battles. Ibid., 12-15.

139. Ibid., 18.

140. Ibid.

141. S. Kobre, *Foundations of American Journalism* (Westport, Conn.: Greenwood Press, 1958), 77.

142. J. Tebbel, *History of the American Newspaper*, (New York: Hawthorn Books, 1963), 35.

143. Commission on the Freedom of the Press (1947).

144. Among Owen's conclusions, he finds that a printing press in the colonial period required only two men for its operation, thus setting the minimum labor requirements for the shop. In addition, Owen looks at other inputs needed for the operation of a printing press, namely, the paper supply and also the technology of the printing press itself.

145. Owen, <u>Economics and Freedom of Expression</u>, 43.

146. Owen, <u>Economics and Freedom of Expression</u>, 44.

147. Alexander Saxton, "Problems of Class and Race in the Origins of the Mass Circulation Press," <u>American Quarterly</u> (Summer 1984).

148. Owen, <u>Economics and Freedom of Expression</u>, 44.

149. "The Media and the First Amendment in a Free Society," <u>Georgetown Law Journal</u> 60 (1972): 867, 879; <u>Miami Herald Publishing Company v. Tornillo</u>, 418 U.S. 241, 249 (1974).

150. Lively and Leahy, "Government and the Media," 913. Late eighteenth-century newspapers published only a scattering of most insignificant advertisements, and publishers considered their publications vehicles for influencing public thought. Emery, <u>The Press and America</u>, 68.

151. "Access to the Press: A Teleological Analysis of a Constitutional Double Standard," <u>George Washington Law Review</u> 50 (1982): 447-48; Don Lively and Mary Ellen Leahy, "Government and the Media: Regulating a First Amendment Value System," <u>University of Florida Law Review</u> 31 (1979): 913.

152. See Lively and Leahy, "Government and the Media," 915. See also Schmidt, <u>Freedom of the Press</u>, 37.

153. Bogen, "Origins of Freedom," 441. As of 1783, ten of the states had made some form of declaration of rights of constitutional provisions protecting liberty of the press, while only two states, Pennsylvania and Vermont, had also mentioned freedom of speech.

154. During the century after the art of printing had been introduced in England in 1476, regulations were enacted to require a printer to obtain a privilege from the king. Later, some printers were granted monopolies for the publication of books dealing with specific subject matter. When the reformation made headway in Europe and found printers in England, however, the king reacted by requiring religious works to be submitted to the church officials before publication. F. Siebert, <u>Freedom of the Press in</u>

England 1476 to 1776 (Urbana: University of Illinois Press, 1952), 23, 25, 31, 35, 38, 46.

155. Ibid. 50-61. The devices of monopolies and limited licensing were constantly supplanted with new laws and regulations that sought both to control content and to regulate commerce.

156. Schmidt, Freedom of the Press, 25.

157. Ibid.

158. Seibert, Freedom of the Press in England, 61, 62.

159. Ibid., 187. Elizabeth's successors had been less and less successful in fending off both religious and secular criticism despite the stationers' companies' attempts to protect their monopoly.

160. Ibid., 260-63. Earlier, with the Restoration, the Printing Act of 1662 had established the licensing system under parliamentary authority with far greater specificity in the requirements for a license, and the Glorious Revolution of 1689 had affected no immediate revolution in the system of licensing. It was the demise of the licensing system that led Blackstone in 1776 to make his famous formulation of freedom of the press in English law: namely, laying no previous restraints on publication. Schmidt, Freedom of the Press, 24.

161. By the late seventeenth century, printers sought protection of their rights of exclusivity in the courts rather than from the king. Secure in existing rights and anxious to secure more business, the stationer's company no longer was zealous in aiding enforcement of the licensing law. Furthermore, the House of Commons perceived the restrictions as driving up the price of books, with no corresponding gain in effectively suppressing offensive ones. For these reasons, the act was not renewed. Seibert, Freedom of the Press in England, 260-63.

162. Schmidt, Freedom of the Press, 25, 26.

163. Seibert, Freedom of the Press in England, 368-74.

164. Ibid., 260-63.

165. W. Blackstone, *Commentaries on the Laws of England*, (London, 1769), 152.

166. Ronald Kahane, "Colonial Origins of Our Free Press," *American Bar Association Journal* 62 (1976): 202-03.

167. Levy, *Legacy of Suppression*, 126-75.

168. This paper was entitled *The New England Courant*. Kahane, "Colonial Origins," 204.

169. Kahane, "Colonial Origins," 204

170. "Media and the First Amendment in a Free Society," 877.

171. Marshall, "Institutional Interpretation," 173.

172. See Bogen, "Origins of Freedom," 444. For a discussion of the dying out of the process of licensing in the colonies, see Duniway, *Development in Massachusetts*, 78-79 and 102-03.

173. Prior to the postal reforms, a postmaster could exclude papers at will or, if he himself conducted one, undercut competitors by franking his own; and, to make matters worse, post riders often alienated customers by charging steep carriage fees. The new regulations established fair and uniform rates for all, with only exchange copies between editors going free; and they also allowed a postmaster a one-fifth commission for collecting money from subscribers and held him financially responsible for any order he himself sent in. See Ruth L. Butler, *Dr. Franklin, Postmaster General* (Garden City, N.J.: Doubleday, Doran & Co., 1928), 56-58.

174. Schlesinger, *Prelude to Independence*, 190-91.

175. Ibid., 192-94. The essays appearing in the newspapers attacked the postal system practices as obstructing and violating a free press.

176. Ibid. David Rabban, review of Emergence of a Free Press, by Leonard Levy, Stanford Law Review, 37 (1985): 795.

177. Ibid.

178. See Duniway, Development in Massachusetts, 121n. However, printers sometimes disregarded all of the government controls. Particular instances of such conduct can be found in L. R. Schuyler, The Liberty of the Press in the American Colonies Before the Revolutionary War (New York: T. Whittaker, 1905), and in Duniway, Development in Massachusetts. The most famous case, of course, was the Zenger case. See Schlesinger, Prelude to Independence, 64-66.

179. Massachusetts in 1753 and New York in 1757 put into effect a stamp duty. Fortunately, the good times enabled the publishers to soften the blow by temporarily raising their subscription rates. Nonetheless, the presses in those states still protested, but these protests failed to arouse the public at large. Nevertheless, the laws were allowed to die at their terminal dates, but the memory of them still rankled in the printing trade when parliament a few years later adopted the far more sweeping Stamp Act. Schlesinger, Prelude to Independence, 65-66.

180. Stewart, The Opposition Press, 460.

181. Ibid., 462.

182. Butler, Dr. Franklin, Postmaster General, 69

183. Duniway, Development in Massachusetts, 74-75.

184. The preamble to the resolution stated that:

> But when, instead thereof, a press is incessantly employed and prostituted to the vilest uses; in publishing the most infamous falsehoods; in partial or false representations of facts; in fomenting jealousies, and exciting discord and disunion among the people; in supporting and applauding the worst of men and worst of measures; and in vilifying and calumniating the best characters, and the best of causes; it then behooves every citizen . . . to

> discountenance and discourage every such licentious illiberal prostituted press.

<u>American Archives</u>, Fourth Series, Volume II, page 12.

Indeed, there was a long tradition and history of the assumption that a legitimate state could not be assaulted by words or speech. Levy, <u>Legacy of Suppression</u>, x. The precariousness of civil order and religious order in the fifteenth through seventeenth centuries in England led government officials to guard against abuse of the press by imposing controls on that press. See, generally, Siebert, <u>Freedom of the Press in England</u>. In eighteenth-century America, however, controls over the press began to relax and printers found themselves enjoying greater liberty. To some extent greater freedom of the press kept pace with the increasing acceptance of religious dissent and the recognition that the American social order rested on firmer foundations. Buel, "Freedom of the Press in Revolutionary America," 68-69.

185. Buel, "Freedom of the Press in Revolutionary America, 82.

186. Fred W. Friendly, Professor of Journalism at Columbia University, raised the question in an editorial published in the <u>Wall Street Journal</u>, 26 January 1979, editorial page.

187. J. M. Smith, <u>Freedom's Fetters</u>, (Ithaca, New York: Cornell University Press, 1956), 426.

188. Schlesinger, <u>Prelude to Independence</u>, 68.

189. Ibid., 69.

190. J. T. Buckinghams, ed., <u>Specimens of Newspaper Literature</u>, vol. 1 (Boston: C. C. Little and J. Brown, 1850), 31.

191. Schlesinger, <u>Prelude to Independence</u>, 80-82.

192. Schlesinger, <u>Prelude to Independence</u>, 72-73.

193. Thomas, <u>History of Printing</u>, vol. 2, 86-95.

194. Schlesinger, Prelude to Independence, 77.

195. Ibid, 80-82. These newspapers, though retaining their regular titles, appeared anonymously.

196. Buckinghams, Specimens of Newspaper Literature, 31

197. Schlesinger, Prelude to Independence, 82.

198. There were at this time twenty-six newspapers in America. The Townshend Acts placed a tax on the importation of paper, which again affected newspapers much as had the Stamp Act. Ibid., 86.

199. In these letters, John Dickinson presented the argument that the act was, in effect, a taxation without representation. Ibid., 89.

200. Ibid., 100-03.

201. Ibid., 95. Particular instances of prosecutions for seditious libel are discussed on pages 96-98.

202. Ibid., 132-34. The progovernment writers seemed to concentrate more on destroying the critics rather than the criticisms. Ibid., 138.

203. Ibid., 108-09.

204. Ibid., 110.

205. In Philadelphia, for instance, a journalistic battle raged over the opinions dealing with the privileged tax status of the extensive lands of the Penn family in 1767. This battle involved the well-to-do Quakers against the Presbyterians. Ibid., 118.

206. Ibid., 119-23.

207. Ibid., 143.

208. Ibid., 164.

209. Ibid., 168.

210. Ibid., 173.

211. See Ibid., 99-182, for a discussion of the content of the newspapers.

212. Ibid.

213. Mott, American Journalism, 46-47.

214. Owen, Economics and Freedom of Expression, 42.

215. Rutland, The Newsmongers, 260-63. By this time the Tories had lost all standing with the public and had little or no access to the press.The debate was now between the three different contending groups of Whigs. The Separationists held that the mother country had committed irreconcilable wrongs. The reconcilers sought a solution short of independence, and the Fence Sitters had not made up their minds yet.

216. Ibid., 261.

217. Owen, Economics and Freedom of Expression, 296-7.

218. Stewart, 630.

219. John Adams, "Dissertation on the Canon and Futile Law" in vol. 3 of The Works of John Adams, ed. Charles Francis Adams (Boston: Little, Brown and Company, 1851), 457.

220. Botein, "Printers," 59.

221. Ibid., 202.

222. G. Nash, "An Economic Interpretation of the American Revolution," *William and Mary Quarterly*, 29 (1974): 199.

223. Schlesinger, *Prelude to Independence*, 241.

224. R. Buel, "Freedom of the Press in Revolutionary America: The Evolution of Libertarianism, 1760-1820," in *The Press and the American Revolution*, ed. Bernard Bailyn and John B. Hench (Worchester: American Antiquarian Society, 1981) 59.

225. Rutland, The *Newsmongers*, 259. To meet these problems, some printers skipped issues or published in reduced size.

226. Ibid., 260.

227. Schlesinger, *Prelude to Independence*, 55, 56.

228. See J. C. Oswald, *Printing in the Americas* (New York: Gregg Publishing Company, 1937), chapter XVI.

229. Ibid., 282-83.

230. Schlesinger, *Prelude to Independence*, 58.

231. Davidson, *Propaganda*, 209.

232. Ibid., 209, 225.

233. Ibid., 226.

234. Ibid.

235. For a discussion, see Schlesinger, *Prelude to Independence*, 223-26. Despite the informal tactics of the patriots aimed at keeping opinions contrary to their own out of print, after 1760 the lower houses in patriot control largely abandoned the

practice of punishing printers for breach of privilege, and ten state constitutions in the revolutionary period explicitly protected a free press. Buel, "Freedom of the Press in Revolutionary America," 60.

236. Robert A. Rutland, <u>The Newsmongers: Journalism in the Life of the Nation. 1690 to 1972</u> (New York: Dial Press, 1973), 60.

237. Weir, "Role of the Newspaper Press," 139.

238. Buel, "Freedom of the Press in Revolutionary America", 72-73. See also David Rabben, review of <u>Emergence of a Free Press</u> (press as a device for uniting the people), 74.

239. Buel, "Freedom of the Press," 73-74.

240. Robert Rutland, <u>Birth of the Bill of Rights</u> (Chapel Hill, North Carolina: University of North Carolina Press, 1955), 27.

241. "Address to the Inhabitants of Quebec 26 October 1775," reprinted in R. Perry and J. Cooper, <u>Sources of Our Liberties</u> (Chicago: American Bar Foundation, 1952), 285.

242. In a document known as the "Continental Association," the Continental Congress declared a comprehensive boycott of Great Britain, Ireland, and the British West Indies. To ensure compliance, the Congress directed that "a committee be chosen in every county, city and town to observe the conduct of all persons touching this association" and, in the event of any violations, to "cause the truth of the case to be published in the <u>Gazette</u>," so that "all such foes to the rights of British America" should be "universally condemned as the enemies of American liberty and all dealings with them ceased." Article XI of the Continental Association, Ibid., 79.

243. Schlesinger, <u>Prelude to Independence</u>, 210-11; Pauline Maier, <u>From Resistance to Revolution</u> (New York: Knopf, 1972); G. C. Smith "An Era of Nonimportation Associations 1768 to 1773,11 <u>William and Mary Quarterly</u> 20 (1969), 92; E. S. Morgan and H. M. Morgan, <u>The Stamp Act Crisis</u>, (Chapel Hill, North Carolina: University of North Carolina Press, 1953).

244. Schlesinger, Prelude to Independence, 281.

245. For a discussion of the perceived impact of the press upon resistance to British regulations and the movement for independence, see Ibid., 285-87.

246. Stewart, Opposition Press, 4.

247. Ibid., 5.

248. Stewart, Opposition Press, 10-11.

249. Smith, Freedom's Fetters, 421.

250. Stewart, Opposition Press, 445.

251. Smith, Freedom's Fetters, 432.

252. Weir, "Role of the Newspaper Press," 99, 100. See also Davidson, Propaganda, 225-45; John Tebbel, The Media in America (New York: Crowell, 1974), 34-50; Mott, American Journalism, 107-08.

253. Stewart, Opposition Press, 13.

254. Edmond S. Morgan, "The American Revolution Considered as an Intellectual Movement," in Paths of American Thought ed. Arthur Schlesinger Jr. and Morton White (Boston: Houghton Mifflen, 1970), 11-33.

255. Merrill Jensen, review of Legacy of Suppression, Harvard Law Review 75, 1 (1961), p. 457.

256. Zechariah Chafee, "Freedom of Speech in War Time," Harvard Law Review 32 (1919): 974. Levy quotes this passage from Chafee's subsequent book, Free Speech in the United States. Chafee's earlier use of this language is significant because it formed part of his disingenuous effort to influence the Supreme Court decisions in the important Espionage Act cases after World War I. See David Rabban, "The Emergence of Modern First Amendment Doctrine," University Chicago Law Review 50 (1983): 1283-1303. In

his dissent in Abrams v. United States, 250 U.S. 616, 630 (1919), the fall after Chafee's article was published, Holmes, without citation, agreed with this historical conclusion.

257. Levy, <u>Legacy of Suppression</u>, 39. But see George Anastaplo, review of <u>Legacy of Suppression: Freedom of Speech and Press in Early American History</u>, by L. Levy, <u>New York University Law Review</u> 39 (1964): 735, rejecting Levy's revisionist account. Anastaplo subsequently expanded on his book review, claiming that Levy misunderstood the close connection between freedom of the press and republican government. G. Anastaplo, <u>The Constitutionalist</u> (Dallas: Southern Methodist University Press, 1971). Anastaplo maintained that, in the generation following the Declaration of Independence, Americans, "groping for a dimly perceived standard of the freedom implicit in their institutions, produced a rich rhetorical tradition, whose significance Levy wrongly disparaged." (103-04).

Even the generally favorable scholarly reviews suggested that Levy overlooked evidence that could have tempered his conclusions. Jensen, <u>U.S. During the Confederation</u>, 457, criticized Levy for limiting himself to a "purely legal" approach, which led him to miss the importance of actual press practices. The law, Jensen maintained, was only a weapon, "not the guiding force," in what was essentially a political battle. Smith reiterated Jensen's complaint that Levy neglected the actual freedom of the press in the colonial period. The willingness of so many people to run the risk of prosecution, Smith concluded, "suggests that there was a 'popular' concept of liberty of expression, no matter how unarticulated in terms of a theoretical definition, which clashed with the legal definition."

Anderson's article, "Origins of the Press Clause," challenges many of the conclusions Levy reaches in <u>Legacy of Suppression</u>. While expressing no view on whether the First Amendment was intended to prevent prosecutions for seditious libel, Anderson effectively refutes Levy's original position that the First Amendment did nothing more than incorporate Blackstone's prohibition against prior restraints (505). Anderson extensively examines the legislative history of the press clause and American discussions of freedom of the press through the Sedition Act of 1978. He concludes "that most of the Framers perceived, however dimly, naively, or incompletely, that freedom of the press was inextricably related to the new republican form of government and would have to be protected if their vision of government by the people was to succeed" (535).

258. Levy, <u>Legacy of Suppression</u>, 104, 201-02.

259. David Rabban, review of <u>Legacy of Suppression</u>, by L. Levy, <u>Yale Law Journal</u>, 72 (1963): 632-33.

260. See Levy, <u>Legacy of Suppression</u>. See also Frank Elliot, <u>The Debates in the Several State Conventions on the Adoption of the Federal Constitution</u>, vol. 2 (1937), which documents that there were frequent references to the abolition of prior censorship in England during the debates over ratification of the Constitution.

261. Levy, <u>Emergence</u>, 348.

262. Levy, <u>Legacy of Suppression</u>, xviii, 297-307.

263. Leonard Levy, <u>Emergence of a Free Press</u>, x.

264. Ibid.

265. Levy points out that in many respects the press enjoyed less actual freedom as the revolution approached than it did throughout most of the colonial period. David Rabban, review of <u>Emergence of a Free Press</u>, by Leonard Levy. Characterizing the period around the revolution, Levy accepts Schlesinger's conclusion that liberty of speech belonged solely to those who spoke the speech of liberty. Levy, <u>Emergence of a Free Press</u>, 173.

266. Levy, <u>Emergence of a Free Press</u>, xii. Obviously, Levy's theories have been much criticized. In a criticism of his book, <u>Emergence of a Free Press</u>, Rabban criticized Levy for judging the libertarianism of the eighteenth-century by a twentieth-century standard. David Rabban, "The Historical Historian: Leonard Levy on Freedom of Expression in Early American History," <u>Stanford Law Review</u> 37 (1985): 795. It is argued that Levy is seriously mistaken and surprisingly historical in assuming that the retention of any concept of seditious libel precludes the existence of meaningful libertarian thought. It is also argued that Levy has difficulty recognizing the benefits of any concept of freedom of political expression, however much leeway it allows for criticism of government, that does not meet his higher and more convincing standard: the total abolition of seditious libel.

Levy has also been criticized for giving short shrift to the influence of such important English thinkers of the times as Bentham. Levy also has been criticized for not giving sufficient attention to public feeling and political climate at the time of the framing of the First Amendment. Levy also has been criticized for ignoring the very language of the First Amendment. Berlin review, <u>Yale Law Journal</u> 72 (1963): 631. See also David Anderson, "The Origins of the Press Clause," <u>UCLA Law Review</u>, 30 (1983): 466.

267. Levy, <u>Emergence of a Free Press</u>, 220-67. See also C. Kenyon, "The Political Thought of the Anti-Federalists," in <u>The Antifederalists</u>, ed. C. Kenyon (Indianapolis: Bobbs-Merrill, 1966), xliv. Alexander Hamilton concluded that, since the federal government had no express or implied powers in this area, it would be unnecessary to include any prohibition against governmental regulation. <u>The Federalist</u>, No. 84. Supporters of this view argued that since seven states already had a bill of rights with free speech and press provisions, and that because this matter was so clearly a state matter, no federal guidelines were needed. (Massachusetts, Maine, Vermont, New Hampshire, North Carolina, Virginia, and Pennsylvania all had bills of rights including free speech and press provisions. See H. Commager, <u>Documents of American History</u> (New York: F. S. Crofts & Co., 1934), 103-09. The Jeffersonian Republicans, however, eventually advocated adoption of the First Amendment, arguing that six states either had no constitution or had no counterpart to the Bill of Rights. S. G. Brown, <u>The First Republicans</u> (Syracuse, New York: Syracuse University Press, 1954), 23-28.

268. Levy, <u>Emergence of a Free Press</u>, xvi-xvii.

269. Ibid., xvii.

270. Dwight Teeter, review of <u>Emergence of a Free Press</u> by Leonard Levy, <u>Reviews in American History</u> XIII (December 1985): 518-25.

271. Levy, <u>Emergence of a Free Press</u>, 268, 273-74, 281.

272. Ibid., 272.

273. Ibid.

274. Emerson, "Colonial Intentions," 737, 751.

275. Schmidt, <u>Freedom of the Press</u>, 38-39, quoting from Baker and Ball, <u>Violence and the Media</u>, staff report to the National Commission on the Causes and Prevention of Violence:

> When the constitution was adopted . . . the individual could make his opinions known by . . . getting a printer to put up a broadside . . . .With relative ease he could have an impact. . A newspaper might have been started with relatively little capital by one whose views were strong enough to demand that they be aired . . . . The media today comprised institutions far different from the press of two centuries ago . . . . The ability of any single man to gain access to the marketplace of ideas has become all but extinct . . . .
>
> "Access to the Press," see n. 176, 448: "The drafters never had reason to anticipate a marketplace of ideas dominated by the view in command of the mass media--one which suffers from a serious lack of diversity largely because many who might otherwise advocate different viewpoints find significant outlets for their expression inaccessible. When the framers drafted the First Amendment, many publications reflected highly partisan viewpoints; a true marketplace of ideas existed in which there was relatively easy access to the channels of communication. The economics of the communications industry has since concentrated the ability to participate effectively in public debate into substantially fewer hands." See also, Miami Herald Publishing Company v. Tornillo, 418 U. S. at 248, 250.

276. <u>Miami Herald Publishing Company v. Tornillo</u>, 418 U.S. at 248.

277. Schmidt, <u>Freedom of the Press</u>, 39-45. Professor Schmidt states that:

> The typical American lives in a city served by a newspaper that is a local monopoly and is owned by the same interests that control one of the local television stations. Both the newspaper and T.V. stations are, in turn, likely to be either part of a centrally controlled chain that holds numerous broadcasting stations and newspapers, or part of a conglomerate corporation with numerous interests that are potentially in conflict with unbiased reporting . . . . Most of the news conveyed by the local paper, and even more of the news that is broadcast in the area, will have from one to two national wire services. . . . Competing daily newspapers have become an oddity. . . . Those

outlets that are independent within a given geographic area are often owned by nation-wide chains and diversified communications conglomerates.

278. Michael Parenti, Democracy for the Few (N.Y. 1988) 157.

279. U.S. Congress, Newspaper Preservation Act: Hearings on H. R. 279 before the Antitrust Subcommittee of the House Committee on the Judiciary, 91st Cong., 1st ses., 1969, 105, 279 (hereafter cited as 1969 Hearings on H. R. 279+-).

280. Ibid., 198. Of those communities served by newspapers, approximately 57 percent had separately owned competing newspapers in 1909 to 1910, compared to 3 percent in 1968.

> According to the "downward spiral" or "vicious cycle" theory, on which the newspaper preservation act is based, the interrelationship of the quality, circulation, and advertising revenues of a newspaper creates a "natural monopoly" that can result in one newspaper cities.

Ibid., 10-12.

281. Owen, Economics and Freedom Expression, 49. Thus, the transition of communications enterprises from persuasion tools to profit instruments has been characterized by a substantial decline in competition and an accompanying increase in concentration. Don Lively and Mary Ellen Leahy, "Government and the Media: Regulating a First Amendment Value System," University of Florida Law Review 31 (1979): 914.

282. See, "Media and the First Amendment, " 893.

283. H. Brucker, Communication is Power, (New York: Oxford University Press, 1973), 333. The hallmarks of newspaper publishing have become newspaper chains, national newspapers, and national wire services. Miami Herald Publishing Company v. Tornillo, 418 U. S. 241, 249 (1974).

According to Professor Schmidt, the emergence of a modern mass media invites analysis that is predicated not on a marketplace of ideas presuming direct citizen participation, but upon recognition of an increasingly centralized mass media with economic and organizational barriers to entry that make individual participation virtually impossible. CBS v. Democratic National Committee, 412 U.S. at 196 (Brennan, J., dissenting).

For other discussions on concentration of the newspaper industry, see Barrow, "The Fairness Act," 685; "Media and the First Amendment," 892, 893.

Newspapers rarely meet the image of an independent editor-publisher daily putting forth his personal interpretation of events and public issues. Instead, newspapers frequently bear the trappings of large-scale business organizations, which are one link in a chain of similar businesses that are components of a conglomerate. Lee C. Bollenger Jr., review of Freedom of the Press v. Public Access, by Benno Schmidt, Columbia Law Review 76 (1976): 1354.

284. Parenti, Democracy for the Few, 157.

285. S. Robert Lichter and Stanley Rothman, "Media and Business Elites," Public Opinion (October/November 1981).

286. Thomas R. Dye, Who's Running America? (Englewood Cliffs, N.J. 1986).

287. "Freedom and Fairness: Regulating the Mass Media," appearing in Report from the Center for Philosophy and Public Policy (Fall 1986).

288. See Associated Press v. United States, 326 U.S. 1, 20 (1945). "Surely a command that the government itself shall not impede the free flow of ideas does not afford nongovernmental combinations if they impose restraints upon that constitutionally guaranteed freedom." In Red Lyon Broadcasting Company v. F.C.C., 395 U.S. 367, 390 (1969), the Court also states that: "It is the purpose of the First Amendment to preserve an uninhibited marketplace of ideas in which truth will ultimately prevail, rather than to countenance monopolization of that market, whether it be by the government itself or a private industry."

289. Barron, "Access to the Press, " 1647-48.

290. Stephen L. Carter, "Technology, Democracy and the Manipulation of Consent," Yale Law Journal 93 (1984): 581.

291. T. White, The Making of the President (N.Y. 1973) 327.

292. Carter, "Technology, Democracy and the Manipulation of Consent," 583.

293. Ibid., 603. According to Professor Pool, the First Amendment creates a presumption that entry by new media cannot be blocked, absent strong government interest. Pool, <u>Technologies of Freedom</u>, 136, 246-47.

294. Barrow, "The Fairness Act," 661.

295. Commission on Freedom of the Press, <u>A Free and Responsible Press</u> (Washington, D.C.: U.S. Government Printing Office, 1947), 80.

296. Schmidt, <u>Freedom of the Press</u>, 37.

297. Ibid.

298. These assumptions are outlined in Johnson and Hoak, "Media Concentration," 276.

299. Johnson and Hoak, "Media Concentration," 275. The Supreme Court has also voiced this attitude in <u>Associated Press v. United States</u>, 326 U.S. at 20.

300. Barrow, "The Fairness Act," 662.

301. Johnson and Hoak, "Media Concentration," 276

302. Ibid.

303. Ibid., 278-79.

304. <u>Associated Press v. United States</u>, 326 U.S. 1, 20 (1945).

305. <u>Times-Picayune Publishing Company v. United States</u>, 345 U.S. 594, 602 (1953).

306. <u>Hale v. F.C.C.</u>, 425 F.2d 556, 561 (D. C. Cir. 1970).

307. 98 S. Ct. 1407, 1426 (1978) (Burger concurring opinion).

308. Ibid.

309. William Doll, "Antitrust Law Meets the Press," The National Law Journal, 15 October 1984.

310. Owen, Economics and Freedom of Expression, 2.

311. Ibid., 12, 13.

312. Ibid. 26-28, 186-87.

313. Leo Bogart, "Newspapers in Transition," appearing in Wilson Quarterly. (Special Issue, 1982), 70.

314. Richard W. Steele, "The Great Debate: Roosevelt, the Media, and the Coming of the War, 1940-41" in The Journal of American History (June 1984).

315. Philip Weiss, "Invasion of the Gannettoids," The New Republic. 2-2-87.

316. Stewart, "Or of the Press," 631.

317. U.S. Constitutional Amendment I.

318. For a discussion of whether the press should be treated differently than the general public, see Van Alstyne, "First Amendment," 10. Among the scholars and judges who have argued that the press be treated differently and better than the general public, Justices Powell and Douglas have been perhaps the most emphatic advocates. Justice Powell has said that in investigating the news, "the press acts as an agent of the public at large." Saxbe v. Washington Post Company, 417 U.S. 483, 863 (1974) (Powell, J. dissenting). Justice Douglas has also said that: "the press has a preferred position in our constitutional scheme, not to enable it to make money, not to set newsmen apart as a favored class, but to bring fulfillment to the public's right to know." Pell v. Procunier, 417 U.S. 817, 839-40 (1974) (Douglas, J. dissenting).

319. Red Lyon Broadcasting Company v. F.C.C., 395 U.S. 367, 686 (1969). See also Joseph Burstyn, Inc. v. Wilson, 343 U.S. 495 (1952). The Supreme Court in Wilson has suggested that a medium's

greater capacity for evil may justify a more permissible scope of control. 343 U.S. at 502, and has concluded that limited spectrum space warrants an ordering of First Amendment rights in the electronic forum. 395 U.S. at 388-90. Such media analysis focuses upon perceived shortcomings or the impact of a given media forum isolated from other media forums.

320. See Robert Bork, "Neutral Principles and Some First Amendment Problems," *Indiana Law Journal* 47(1971): 1.

321. 274 U.S. 357, 374-75 (1927) (Brandeis, J., concurring).

322. Blasi, "Checking Value, " 528.

323. Nimmer, "Is Freedom of the Press a Redundancy," 653-56. John Stewart Mill is among the most influential advocates of individuality in the history of political philosophy, yet he considered it a social rather than personal value. See H. Magid, "John Stewart Mill," in *History of Political Philosophy*, 2d ed., ed. Leo Strauss and Joseph Cropsey (London: J. W. Parker & Son, 1972), 415. As a utilitarian, Mill specifically disclaimed the belief that freedom is inherently valuable. John Stewart Mill, *On Liberty*, ed. D. Spitz (New York: Norton, 1975). On the contrary, for Mill, the value of freedom lies in its potential for improving the human condition in social progress, which he considered both possible and desirable, but not inevitable. Magid, "John Stewart Mill," 739.

324. See, R. Jebb, ed., *Commentary to John Milton*, (Cambridge: Oxford University Press, 1918).

325. The Supreme Court, for example, quoted Mill extensively in New York Times Company v. Sullivan, 376 U.S. 254 (1964).

326. Mill, *On Liberty*, 18.

327. "Thomas Jefferson, James Madison, and the other founding fathers were children of the enlightenment. They believed above all else in a power of reason, in the search for truth, in progress and the ultimate perfectibility of man. Freedom of inquiry and liberty of expression were deemed essential to the discovery in spread of truth, for only by the endless testing of debate could error be exposed, truth emerge, and man enjoy the opportunities for human progress."

328. See Cox, "Freedom of Expression in the Burger Court," 2.

329. *Journals of the Continental Congress*, 1 (1776): 104, quoted in Near v. Minnesota, 283 U.S. 697, iii (1931).

330. Zechariah Chafee, *Free Speech in the United States* (Cambridge: Harvard University Press, 1942), 31.

331. Alexander Meiklejohn, *Free Speech and its Relation to Self-Government* (New York: Harper & Row, 1972) 26, 27. My theory of the press clause focuses on the dissemination part of Meiklejohn's theory.

Some modern scholars do not automatically accept the argument that truth and reason will necessarily prevail from the competition of ideas. Frederick Schauer, *Free Speech: A Philosophical Inquiry* (Cambridge: Cambridge University Press, 1982), believes that the argument of truth does direct our attention to the fallibility of human judgments and the necessity of constantly keeping open the channels of criticism. Schauer prefers the marketplace of ideas concept over the selection of truth by government, not so much because the former has proved itself competent but because the latter is incompetent for the task.

332. 250 U.S. 616, 630 (1919).

333. 274 U.S. 357, 375 (1927) (Brandeis, J., concurring). This view was also restated in *Red Lyon Broadcasting Company v. F.C.C.*, 395 U.S. 367, 390 (1969): "A free flow of information in an uninhibited marketplace of ideas will produce truth."

334. Associated Press v. United States, 326 U.S. 1, 20 (1945).

335. For example, see *Mills v. Alabama*, 384 U.S. 214, 218 (1966) "Whatever differences may exist about interpretations of the First Amendment, there is practically universal agreement that a major purpose of that amendment was to protect the free discussion of government affairs."

336. *Buckley v. Valeo*, 424 U.S. 1, 14 (1976): "The First Amendment affords the broadest protection to such political expression . . . "; *City of Chicago v. Mosley*, 408 U.S. 92, 95

(1972): "To permit the continued building of our politics . . . Red Lyon Broadcasting Company v. F.C.C., 395 U.S. 367, 390 (1969): "The Essence of Self-Government"; Roth v. United States, 354 U.S. 476, 484 (1957): "The protection given speech and press was fashioned to assure unfettered interchange of ideas for the bringing about of political and social changes desired by the people.".

337. Herbert v. Lando, 441 U.S. 153, 184 (Power, J., concurring).

338. Some scholars hold that the First Amendment's sole purpose is to support democracy. See Alexander Meiklejohn, Political Freedom: The Constitutional Powers of the People (New York: Harper & Row, 1960); Bork, "Neutral Principles." Even those writers who reject the exclusiveness of this view of the First Amendment's purpose acknowledge the importance of the First Amendment to the public's participation in political decision making. See Emerson, The System of Freedom, 7.

339. Meiklejohn, Free Speech and Self-Government, 26, 27, 88, 89.

340. See Meiklejohn, Political Freedom+-; Meiklejohn, "The First Amendment is an Absolute," Supreme Court Review 1961: 245.

341. Meiklejohn, Political Freedom, 75.

342. Nimmer, "Is Freedom of the Press a Redundancy," 653. ("The informing and opinion shaping function of the press is unquestioned.")

343. Ibid.

344. Berkshire Cablevision v. Burke, 52 U.S.L.W. 2181 (1983).

345. These findings were made in a study by University of Iowa Professor Samuel L. Becher of the 1982 Iowa gubernatorial race.

346. See John Hart Ely, Democracy and Distrust (Cambridge: Harvard University Press, 1980); John Hart Ely, "The Supreme Court, 1977 Term," Harvard Law Review, 92 (1978): 5; John Hart Ely, "Toward a Representation Reinforcing Mode of Judicial Review" Maryland Law Review 37 (1978): 451.

Some scholars have also written that the First Amendment free press clause should serve an equalizing function. See Robert Maister, "Journalistic Silence in Governmental Speech: Can Institutions Have Rights?" Harvard Civil Rights - Civil Liberties Law Review 16 (1981): 319. Such a function would require the press to act as a forum for oppressed or minority groups or to conduct investigations into systematic oppression. Thus, when performing such a function, the press would be given special rights.

The value of a free press in promoting participation in government by citizens was particularly noticed by Justice Frankferter, who wrote:

> In the years between the wars few things were more disturbing than the number of citizens who gave up the effort to understand our problems . . Education means the power to reduce the number of citizens who give up the effort of disinterested and responsible understanding ., for where the effort is made, there citizens are found: and where citizens are found, responsibility is squarely forced upon a statesman to explain, if need be to justify, the policy he proposes.

F. Frankferter, "There is no Middle Way," Saturday Review of Literature, 26 October 1941, 21.

347. Emerson, The System of Freedom, 6-7.

348. Leonard, Power of the Press, 6.

349. In Technologies of Freedom, Pool presents an even broader issue: In a democracy dependent upon the free exchange of ideas, what is to become of that system if society grows dependent upon a communication system that is extensively regulated or monopolized? A similar question is what is to happen to freedom if society grows dependent upon a communication system that is overly concentrated and monopolistic? The heart of Pool's thesis is that resource availability ought to determine the degree of regulation. To the extent that resources for an important communications medium are genuinely scarce or are monopolized, governmental regulation may be necessary, but only to ensure open access. To the extent that a communications medium is decentralized and dispersed and is thus widely available, little or no governmental regulation is required. Thus, regulation is a last recourse according to Pool, legitimate only if an important communications medium is truly monopolistic. These principles make it clear that Pool is a pluralist: they reflect his goal of ensuring that all speakers have maximum opportunity to speak (9-10, 234-40, 246).

350. Berkshire Cablevision v. Burke, 52 U.S. L.W. 2181 (1983).

351. Eric Foner, Tom Paine and Revolutionary America (New York: Oxford University Press, 1976), 92.

352. Roscoe Pound, "Sociological Jurisprudence," in Jurisprudence, ed. Ervin Pollack (Columbus: Ohio State University Press 1979), 161. According to Pound, the law reflects and reconciles three types of interests: individual, public, and social. According to Pound: "I think of law as in one sense a highly specialized form of social control in a developed politically organized society--a social control through the orderly application of the force of such a society" 635.

353. Professor Stone argues that in democratic countries free expression should approach absoluteness because it is "a vital prerequisite to the formation and expression of human demands concerning the exercise of political authority. Indeed, insofar as we recognize that the function of law in a free community is the satisfaction of human demands for the time being, it is proper to point out that this function must be frustrated insofar as freedom of speech is not permitted to articulate those demands." Julius Stone, The Province and Function of Law (Cambridge: Harvard University Press, 1950), 520-21.

354. Hannah Arendt, The Human Condition (Chicago: University of Chicago Press, 1958), 176.

355. Peter Schneider, "Social Rights and the Concept of Human Rights," in Political Theory in the Rights of Man, ed. D. D. Raphael (Bloomington: Indiana University Press, 1967), 81.

356. Karl W. Deutsch, Nationalism and Social Communication: An Inquiry into the Foundations of Nationality, 2d ed. (Cambridge, Massachusetts: Wiley, 1966).

357. Arendt, The Human Condition, 208.

358. John Dewey, Freedom and Culture (New York: Paragon Books, 1939), 6.

359. Franklyn S. Haiman, Speech and Law in a Free Society (Chicago: University of Chicago Press, 1981), 3.

360. Dewey, *Freedom and Culture*, 13.

361. Ibid., 23.

362. Levy, *Emergence of a Free Press*, x.

363. See, generally, Lawrence Goodwin, *Democratic Promise: The Populist Moment* in America (London: Oxford University Press, 1976).

364. Weir, "Role of the Newspaper," 102.

365. Ibid., 127.

366. Ibid., 129.

367. Ibid., 130.

368. While this value is primarily a sociological one, it has gained legal recognition. *New York Times v. Sullivan*, 376, U.S. 254, 301 (1964) (Goldberg, J., concurring); Commission on Freedom of the Press, *Free and Responsible Press*, 113; Barron, "Access to the Press," 1650.

369. Haiman, *Speech and Law*, 6.

370. See Emerson, *The System of Freedom of Expression*, 6, 7.

371. 274 U.S. 357, 375 (1927).

372. Barron, "Access to the Press," 1650.

373. Blasi, "Checking Value," 550. There may also be a safety valve function for the audience as well as the speaker. See *Richmond Newspapers, Inc. v. Virginia*, 448 U.S. 555, 571 (1980) (plurality opinion Burger, C. J.): "Without an awareness that society's responses to criminal conduct are underway, natural human reactions of outrage and protest are frustrated and may manifest themselves in some form of vengeful self-help, as indeed they did regularly in the activities of vigilante committees on our frontiers."

Professor Emerson suggests as a fourth, separate function that of "promoting orderly social change" or "maintaining a balance between stability and change." See Emerson, "First Amendment," 428.

Professor Bork, on the other hand, argues that since the safety valve function raises only issues of prudence, it therefore raises issues to be determined by the legislature or the executive. Bork, "Neutral Principles," 25.

374. This value is discussed in Blasi, "Checking Value, " 521.

375. Stewart, "Or of the Press, " 634.

376. <u>Branzburg v. Hayes</u>, 408 U.S. 655, 722 (1972).

The Court has continued to stress this structural, adversarial role. As Justice Brennan stated in <u>Richmond Newspapers, Inc. v. Virginia</u>, "The First Amendment embodies more than a commitment to free expression and communicative interchange for their own sakes: it has a structural role to play in securing and fostering a republican form of self-government." 448 U.S. 555, 587 (1980). Thus, this checking value envisions the press as an independent check on the government.

377. Blasi, "Checking Value.

378. Ibid., 527.

379. According to Blasi, the "checking value is concerned not with the general process of selecting the best persons for office but with the narrower task of preventing abuses of the public trust." Ibid., 584.

380. Ibid., 542.

381. Schmidt, <u>Freedom of the Press</u>, 58-59. According to Schmidt, the Vietnam War was critical in changing the attitude of journalists toward their government: "The radical perspective of journalist I. F. Stone ('every government is run by liars and nothing they say should be believed') became an accepted premise of reporting about the war." Schmidt also states that the growth of serious radical and countercultural movements led to an

adversarial role between press and government. As the press reported about activities of legal disobedience by these groups in the 1960s, law enforcement officials found journalists with information about militant groups to be tempting sources of information. (60) This wave of subpoenas and investigations left journalists with the attitude that government wished to cut off its flow of information. As a result, many journalists viewed cooperation with law enforcement authorities as a threat to their ability to investigate. (60)

382. For a discussion of the press' role during the Vietnam War, see Kathleen J. Turner, Lyndon Johnson's Dual War: Vietnam and the Press (Chicago 1985).

383. Nimmer, "Is Freedom of the Press a Redundancy," 653. Professor Nimmer, in addressing that question, first looked at the functions and rationale for protections of speech and press. To evaluate the significance of the differences between the speech and free functions, Professor Nimmer then considered situations in which the forces of speech and press pull in the same direction and those situations in which they pull in opposite directions. (654)

384. Schauer, Free Speech, 127. Schauer warns us not to confuse free speech with the conditions necessary for its expression. According to Schauer, the two are interrelated, but freedom and the requisites for its exercise are separate problems.

385. One author has said that the value of free expression "rests on its deep relation to self-respect arising from autonomous self-determination without which the life of the spirit is meager and slavish." David A. J. Richards, "Free Speech and Obscenity Law: Toward a Moral Theory of the First Amendment," University of Pennsylvania Law Review 123 (1974): 45, 62.

386. Nimmer, "Is Freedom of the Press a Redundancy," 654. ("To be sure, the individual contributor to the press makes variant self-fulfillment by the publication of his work. But for the press qua press, apart from the individual pamphleteer, it is unlikely that this is a significant factor.")

387. For a discussion of this liberty theory of free speech, see C. Edwin Baker, "Scope of the First Amendment Freedom of Speech," UCLA Law Review 26 (1978): 964. In a later paper, Professor Baker discusses the view that since the press is a commercial enterprise, its speech lacks the individual liberty and self-realization aspects of speech that justify its constitutional

protection for individuals. Thus, the value of individual liberty is not closely connected with the activities of the press. See C. Edwin Baker, "Press Rights and Government Power to Structure the Press," University of Miami Law Review 34 (1980): 819.

388. 417 U.S. 817 (1974).

389. 435 U.S. 765 (1978).

390. Gerald Gunther, "Learned Hand and the Origins of Modern First Amendment Doctrine," Stanford Law Review 27(1975): 862. "There is an individual interest, the need of many men to express their opinions on matters vital to them if life is to be worth living, and a social interest in the attainment of truth, so that the country may not only adopt the wisest course of action but carry it out in the wisest way." Chafee, Free Speech in the United States, 33.

391. Chafee, Free Speech in the United States, 31-35.

392. Baker, "Press Rights," 859.

393. Saxbe v. Washington Post Company, 417 U.S. 817, 862. Justice Powell relied upon Professor Chafee's reservation that "the guarantee of freedom of speech and press protects two kinds of interests." 417 U.S. at 862. In his dissent in Saxbe, Powell also agreed with Justice Stewart's major premise that neither any news organization nor reporters as individuals have constitutional rights superior to those of the general public. 417 U.S. at 857. However, Powell did not view this concession as fatal because of the two kinds of interests protected by the First Amendment--i.e., individualistic values and the societal function. Justice Stewart viewed the plaintiff's claim in Saxbe as staking out an area of special press privilege, thus implicating only the individualist values of the First Amendment. Powell, however, insisted the plaintiff's claim in Saxbe implicated systematic, process-related concerns--the societal function of the First Amendment. Lillian R. BeVier, "Justice Powell and the First Amendment's Societal Function: A Preliminary Analysis," Virginia Law Review 68 (1982): 177. According to Powell, the plaintiffs in Saxbe were seeking constitutional protection not as individuals but as agents of the public at large because "the press performs a crucial function in effecting the societal purpose of the First Amendment." 417 U.S. at 863.

394. Ibid.

395. BeVier, "Justice Powell," 183-84. "Yet, the Saxbe dissent demonstrates that when the First Amendment is called upon to guarantee the integrity of democratic political processes, rights may be conferred legitimately on a distinct group according to the needs of processes, quite apart from the merits for inherent worth of the group as persons."

396. Melvin B. Nimmer, Freedom of Speech (New York: Mathew Bender and Company, 1984), 4-41.

397. Richmond Newspapers, Inc. v. Virginia, 448 U.S. 555, 588 (1980) (Brennan, J., concurring).

398. Gerald Gunther, Cases and Materials On Constitutional Law (New York: Foundation Press, 1980), 1108.

399. Isaiah Berlin, Four Essays on Liberty (New York: Oxford University Press, 1969), 122. Isaiah Berlin held the Kantian view that the individual must retain control over some private sphere beyond a government's control where that person can be free. See Charles Taylor, "What's Wrong With Negative Liberty," in The Idea of Freedom, ed. Alan Ryan (New York: Oxford University Press, 1979), 176. Berlin saw freedom of speech as an individual negative liberty--the freedom from government restrictions. Berlin valued this liberty because of its contribution to individual dignity and freedom.

400. Berlin, Four Essays, 130. Berlin separated liberty of expression from the issue of self-government:

> There is no necessary connection between individual liberty and democratic rule. The answer to the question "who governs me?" is logically distinct from the question "how far does government interfere with me?" It is in this difference that the great contrast between the two concepts of negative and positive liberty in the end consists.

> Thus, Berlin draws a line between the area of private life and that of public authority.

401. Berlin, Four Essays on Liberty, 126.

402. See Meiklejohn, "First Amendment is an Absolute, " 245; William J. Brennan, Jr., "The Supreme Court and the Meiklejohn Interpretation of the First Amendment," Harvard Law Review 79 (1965): 1. The First Amendment, in Meiklejohn's view, constitutes the repository of self-governing powers that are immune from governmental regulation. These reserved "self-governing" powers are concerned not with a private right but with a public power. Meiklejohn argues that the First Amendment is not concerned with a private freedom to speak, but rather with the freedom of those expressions by which we govern. Thus, in Meiklejohn's view the First Amendment protects the presence of self-government. Meiklejohn holds that the First Amendment exists primarily as a power by which people can effectively govern themselves.

Bork believes, along with Meiklejohn, that self-government constitutes the only legitimate value of the First Amendment. Bork, "Neutral Principles," Bork views the First Amendment as guaranteeing the derivative rights--rights derived from the governmental processes established by the Constitution.

403. Meiklejohn, "First Amendment is an Absolute, " 252.

404. Bork stated that speech confers four benefits: (1) the development of the faculties of the individual; (2) the happiness to be derived from engaging in the activity; (3) the provision of a safety valve for society; (4) the discovery and spread of political truth. Bork believed, however, that free speech protection could not be premised on the first two values. Bork then analyzed the process-protective nature of the Constitution and saw that the Constitution was primarily concerned with protecting the process of self-government. Therefore, Bork sought to protect speech only as it contributed to self-government. What Bork should have done, however, is not only to separate the benefit that speech confers, but also to separate the different protections the speech and press clause guarantees.

405. 457 U.S. 596 (1982). In Globe Newspaper Company, the Court established that the press and public have a right of access to criminal trials guaranteed by the First Amendment. The Court held that a state statute barring press and public access to criminal trials of alleged sex offenders during the testimony of minor victims infringed on the First Amendment right of access.

406. For a discussion of freedom of speech as a negative liberty, see the discussion on Dworkin in Maister, "Journalistic Silence and Governmental Speech," 334-40.

The original provisions of the Constitution conferred liberties in the positive sense. As defined by Isaiah Berlin, the positive sense of the word liberty "derives from the wish on the part of the individual to be his own master." Berlin, Four Essays on Liberty, 131. The Constitution created democratic processes by which the American people could be their own masters. The press clause is one such process and is essential in order for the public to govern themselves. Also, the self-governing rationale provides the only legitimate justification for the press clause. This argument is accepted by theorists ranging from Bork and Meiklejohn to Justice Stewart in his fourth estate role. Justice Stewart believes that, while most of the other provisions in the Bill of Rights protect specific liberties of individuals, the free press clause is a structural provision extending protection to an institution. Stewart, "Or of the Press," 633.

Other authors and judges suggest that the press clause should be seen as a positive liberty. Justice Stewart stated that the free press guaranty is a structional provision of the constitution. Stewart, "Or of the Press," 633. The quote has also suggested, though not precisely, that the institutional press may claim a protected status in the constitutional system of free expression as a third-party representative of the public. See Branzburg v. Hayes, 408 U.S. 665, 725-26 (1972) (Stewart, D., dissenting); Houchins v. K. Q. E. D., Inc., 438 U.S. 1, 30-34 (1978) (Stevens, J., dissenting); Pell v. Procunier, 417 U.S. at 817. This function of the press obviously is closely intertwined with the ability of the public to self-govern. Another author has stated that the press, in serving an equalizing function, is a necessary institution to offset the power of government and to help "outside groups" gain access to the political process. Maister, "Journalistic Silence and Governmental Speech," 355-56. In this view, the press becomes part of the social conflict and takes part in politicizing the government. See also pages 363-76 for a discussion of the political roles that the institutional press may play.

Thus, if the prime justification for the press is in its role within the political arena, the freedom of the press clause must be viewed as protecting a positive liberty.

407. Ely discusses his free speech theory in a chapter entitled, "Cleaning the Channels of Political Change," in Democracy and Distrust. See also the discussion in Maister, "Journalistic Silence and Governmental Speech." 363-67.

408. Ely, Democracy and Distrust, 112.

409. Ibid., chapters 3-6. The counterdoctrine, developed by the Warren Court, is that the Constitution requires that the courts correct defects in the representative process by reinforcing the representation of those underrepresented minorities which have been excluded from the pluralist political process. Maister, "Journalistic Silence and Governmental Speech," 364.

410. Bezanson "New Free Press Guarantee," 732.

411. Baker, "Press Rights," 825.

412. Ibid., 827.

413. Stewart, "Or of the Press," 633.

414. Ibid., 634. "It is also a mistake to suppose that the only purpose of the Constitutional guarantee of a free press is to ensure that a newspaper will serve a neutral forum for debate, a marketplace for ideas." According to Justice Stewart, the marketplace of ideas concept gives insufficient weight to the institutional autonomy of the press.

415. 418 U.S. 232 (1974). The issue in <u>Gertz</u> was the extent of press liability for defamatory statements about private individuals. The <u>Gertz</u> case is an example of a Supreme Court decision interpreting the press clause as an institutional protection or at least displaying an increasing willingness to depart from a unitary free speech and free press right. Rooney, "Freedom of the Press," 38. In its decision, the Court abandoned its traditional free speech analysis, which had focused on the content of any given expression and on the character of the purported evil presented. In place of the traditional analysis, the layout emphasized institutional considerations unrelated to context.

416. 448 U.S. 555 (1980) (Brennan, J. concurring).

417. Ibid., 587.

418. Pool, <u>Technologies of Freedom</u>, 9-10.

419. Ibid.

420. Ibid., 246.

421. U.S. Constitutional Amendment 1. "Congress shall make no law . . . abridging the freedom of speech, or of the press . . . ." Since there is a strong presumption that words used in a constitution were shown for a purpose and are, therefore, not redundant, it follows that the framers intended to establish two separate freedoms. Nimmer, "Is Freedom of the Press a Redundancy," 639-40.

422. The Papers of T. Jefferson, vol. 1, ed. J. Boyd (Princeton, Princeton University Press, 1950), 363.

423. Anderson, "Origins of the Press Clause, " 490. See also Bernard Schwartz, The Bill of Rights: A Documentary History, vol. 1 (New York: Chelsea House Publishers, 1971) 228-30.

424. The fourth estate model seeks to establish the press as an ombudsman to safeguard the public by documenting official abuse. Blasi, "Checking Value." Assigning this responsibility to the institutional press conveniently limits and identifies the group of people who can exercise the rights of the ombudsman. Society can then afford to give the ombudsman certain tools--i.e., access to government information and testimonial and reporting privileges-that would be too costly to give to every individual.

Professor Lange, however, argues that two dangers are posed by such an interpretation of the press guarantee. First, he believes that an institutional definition of the press could result in the imposition of First Amendment duties as well as rights. Second, he argues that mere speech with no 'distinct institutional identification--and now without claim to immediate theoretical alliance with the press--. . . may find it more difficult to stand up against the constraints which a mass society inevitably finds it convenient to impose." Lange, "Speech and Press Clauses," 107-13.

425. Schlesinger, Prelude to Independence, ch. 9.

426. Journals of the Continental Congress, 1774-1789, (Washington, 1904-37) 1:25-26 and 43-51.

427. See John Borger, "News Gathering Versus Privacy: Tension Around the First Amendment," Hamline Law Review, (1978): 1, 4.

428. Some justices find no substantive difference between the speech and press clauses of the First Amendment. Chief Justice Burger seems to take this position, and he is supported by Justices White, Blackman, and Renquist. Others believe that the press is entitled to broad constitutional protection because the press clause protects the press as an institution. Justice Stewart is the major proponent of this position. See Houchin S. V. K. Q. E. D., Inc., 438 U.S. 1, 17 (1978) (Stewart, J., concurring); Branzburg v. Hayes, 408 U.S. 665, 727 (1972) (Stewart, J., dissenting). Others hold that the press clause was designed to preserve the societal function of the press: the collection, analysis, and dissemination of information. This appears to be the position of Justices Powell, Stevens, Marshall, and Brennan. See Gannett Company v. DePasquale, 443 U.S. 368 (1979); Zurcher v. Stanford Daily, 436 U.S. 547 (1978); Richmond Newspapers, Inc. v. Virginia, 448 U.S. 555, 587 (1980) (Brennan, J., concurring).

429. Columbia Broadcasting System, Inc. v. Democratic National Committee, 412 U.S. 94, 124 (1973) ("Editing . . . is what editors are for.") See also Miami Herald Publishing Company v. Tornillo, 418 U.S. 241, 258 (1974) ("It is yet to be demonstrated how government regulation of this crucial process can be exercised consistent with the First Amendment guarantees . . . ") This function is protected even against discovery by a private plaintiff in a defamation action. See Herbert v. Landow. See also, Miami Herald Publishing Company v. Tornillo, 418 U.S. 214.

430. Miami Herald Publishing Company v. Tornillo, 418 U.S. 241.

431. Schmidt, Freedom of the Press, 237-38. According to Schmidt, the prime value of the First Amendment is the maintenance and preservation of editorial autonomy. Schmidt, Freedom of the Press, 31. There are several problems, however, with viewing the First Amendment primarily as protecting editorial autonomy. Media organizations rarely meet the image of an independent editor-publisher putting forth his personal interpretations of events and public issues. Essentially, the problems with the autonomy concept are twofold: first, is anyone's autonomy or dignity seriously diminished or implicated in a context where the principal motivation of the act is stock value; and second, if so, whose dignity is being implicated? Lee C. Bollinger, Jr., review of Freedom of the Press v. Public Access, by Benno C. Schmidt, Columbia Law Review 76 (1976): 1354.

432. 418 U.S. at 258.

433. Time, Inc. v. Hill, 385 U.S. 374 (1967).

434. Gertz v. Robert Welch, Inc., 418 U.S. 323 (1974); New York Times Company v. Sullivan, 376 U.S. 254 (1964).

435. Talley v. California, 362 U.S. 60, 64 (1960); Lovell v. City of Griffin, 303 U.S. 444, 452 (1938).

436. United States v. O'Brien, 391 U.S. 367 (1968).

437. New Times, Inc. v. Arizona Board of Regents, 110 Ariz. 367, 371, 519 P.2d 169, 173 (1974).

438. Lovell v. Griffin, 303 U.S. 444, 452 (1938), cited in Southern N.J. Newspapers v. State of N.J., 542 F. Supp. 173, 182 (1982).

439. The taxation and regulation cases also hold that the press is not to be singled out for taxation or regulation which may impinge on its function of dissemination. The Minneapolis Star and Tribune case holds that the press cannot be singled out for regulation or taxation in its function of publishing and disseminating the news. Minneapolis Star & Tribune v. Minnesota Commissioner of Revenue, 103 S. Ct. 1365 (1983).

440. 52 U.S.L.W. 4612 (1984).

441. 53 U.S.L.W. 1143 (1985).

442. For a discussion of the history underlying the right of news gathering, see Burger, "News Gathering Verses Privacy," 6-13.

443. 408 U.S. 665 (1972). The three cases consolidated for review in Branzburg involved reporters who had covered activities of Black Panthers or of local drug users. Each reporter was subpoenaed by a grand jury to testify concerning information he had obtained in confidence in the course of his news gathering activities. Justice White's opinion (Justice White was joined by Chief Justice Burger and by Justice Blackman) conceded that "without some protection for seeking out the news, freedom of the

press could be eviscerated." 408 U.S. at 681. Nonetheless, Justice White required the reporters to answer the grand jury's questions. In Zemel v. Rusk, 408 U.S. at 702, Justice White equated the press's right to gather news with the public's right to obtain information; reporters, like other citizens, would have to cooperate with the grand jury. 408 U.S. at 702. Reporters could seek protection from the court only if the grand jury investigation was "undertaken not for the purpose of law enforcement but to disrupt a reporter's relationship with his news sources". 408 U.S. at 707-08.

444. In the companion cases of Pell v. Procunier, 417 U.S. 817 (1974) and Saxbe v. Washington Post Company, 417 U.S. 843 (1974), the Court rejected attacks by news media representatives against what they perceived as an interference with their right to gather news and upheld state and federal prison regulations which banned all personal interviews between news reporters and individually designated prison inmates. The majority of the Court in both cases treated the central issue as one of affirmative access to public information.

445. Richmond Newspapers, Inc. held that the First Amendment guarantees the right of the public and press to attend criminal trials. 448 U.S. 555 (1980).

446. 457 U.S. 596 (1982).

447. The Court held that the First Amendment includes, "those rights that, while not unambiguously enumerated, are nonetheless necessary to the enjoyment of other First Amendment rights . . . . Underlying the First Amendment right of access to criminal trials is the common understanding that a major purpose of that amendment was to protect the free discussion of governmental affairs." 457 U.S. at 604.

448. See Nimmer, Freedom of Speech, 4-58.

449. 408 U.S. 665 (1972). See Herbert v. Landow, 441 U.S. 153 (1979), which rejected a claim of First Amendment privilege in the reediting communications among editors.

450. The Branzburg dissenters leave the newsmen's privilege open for application in future cases, but with no clear indication as to the circumstances in which it may be invoked.

451. Houchins v. K.Q.E.D., Inc., 438 U.S. 1, 32 n. 22 (1978) (Stevens, J., dissenting). Indeed, according to Professor Nimmer, it is only because the absence of such a newsman's privilege would deter the ability to gather information that the privilege itself has a constitutional base. Nimmer, Freedom of Speech, 4-64.

452. See John Shattuck and Fritz Byers, "An Egalitarian Interpretation of the First Amendment," Harvard Civil Rights--Civil Liberties Law Review, 16 (1981): 377. According to the authors, the press must perform the role of keeping constant surveillance over the government's activities. To do this, the press must have a right to seek and publish government information which is not accessible to the public. To perform this role, the press must have the freedom to pursue information and to engage in investigative journalism.

453. One aspect of the media's role is its importance in the marketplace of ideas. See, Red Lyon Broadcasting Company v. F.C.C., 395 U.S. 367 (1969); New York Times Company v. Sullivan, 376 U.S. 254 (1964); Associated Press v. United States, 326 U.S. 1 (1945). Media provides forums in this marketplace through which individuals and groups may express their opinions. Direct involvement of citizens in government is implicit in the marketplace theory. Although control of the government by the representative process is indirect, a free press helps bring about the political and social changes desired by the citizens. "Media and the First Amendment," 884, 85. while the marketplace theory carries the image of a single forum for ideas, in reality the marketplace is many forums. A distinction must be made between a guaranty of the opportunity to be heard in a forum and a guaranty that there will be a multitude of forums for expression. The former is the primary objective of the First Amendment theory of Jerome Barron. Jerome Barron, "An Emerging First Amendment Right of Access to the Media?" George Washington Law Review 30 (1969): 487.

454. The right of access proposed by Jerome Barron does not serve this function of natural selection of ideas. With a right of access, editors are forced to print certain opinions, without being able to gauge the degree of acceptance of those opinions and who holds those opinions. In a sense, a right of access creates a superficial outlet for the ideas. Furthermore, a right of access impinges upon the editorial integrity of a newspaper, while a natural forum does not.

455. Pool, Technologies of Freedom, 238.

456. Nimmer, *Freedom of Speech*, 1-16.

457. "The Press Under Pressure," *Wieman Reports*, April 1948.

458. See *United States v. Dennis*, 183 F.2d 201, 207 (2d Cir. 1950). Judge Learned Hand stated that the airing of dissident views "may convince the officials themselves, and in any event it may rouse up a body of contrary opinion to which they will yield, or which will displace them."

459. This industry structure of independent and competitive media is also important so that the government acts according to the wishes of the majority and not according to the wishes of a few. Free and open debate on issues of public importance is necessary for the healthy functioning of a democracy. Therefore, as the power to shape opinion or to decide which opinions are heard is concentrated in fewer hands, the democracy may grow less and less healthy.

460. Pool, *Technologies of Freedom*.

461. Emerson, *The System of Freedom of Expression*, 629.

One author has stated that the First Amendment should be interpreted "teleologically." See "Access to the Press," 430. Such an interpretation would look to the spirit of the press clause and would then seek to uphold that spirit. For instance, if the First Amendment is meant to give the public a diverse source of ideas, then the First Amendment would not protect activity of speakers that decreases or limits the diversity of viewpoints expressed or the flow of ideas to the public. In a sense then, rights are not given to individuals but to the act of communication and to the communicative process. Likewise, the revised marketplace theory might also fit into such an interpretation.

462. Chafee, *Free Speech in the United States*, 559.

463. Professor Owen conceives of media firms as "gatekeepers" that control the flow of news and opinion and screen out ideas inimical to their economic interests or otherwise uncongenial to them. Owen, *Economics and Freedom of Expression*, 12-13. Given this gate-keeper function, Owen argues that concentration in the media entails a reduction, potentially to dangerously low levels, in the diversity of views disseminated to the public.

464. Thus, there would be no need for offensive access rights.

465. Such concentration also reduces the participation of the public in the political process. Thus, concentration reduces the representative nature of our democracy.

466. See Section III above.

467. This trend began in the progressive era. See Paul Murphy, "Near v. Minnesota in the Context of Historical Developments," Minnesota Law Review 66 (1981): 95, 133-37. It has also taken such a role since Watergate.

468. Fisher, "Free Speech and High Tech," 983.

469. Pool, Technologies of Freedom, 9-10, 234-40.

470. According to Pool, under monopoly conditions common carrier (that is, structural) regulation is preferable to direct content regulation or government ownership. Ibid., 246.

471. Thus, despite his support of the absolutist view of the First Amendment throughout much of the book, Pool seems quite willing to accept structural regulation if the ends that he seeks would be fostered.

472. Pool never explicitly states that the newspaper industry may have crossed the line from a regulation-free status to one with duties of a common carrier, but in his final chapter he does seem to accept that conclusion. Ibid., 238-39.

473. See Mark S. Nadel, "Electrifying the First Amendment," Cardozo Law Review 5 (1984): 531, 536.

474. Pool, Technologies of Freedom, 81. According to Pool, all media entities must be accorded an unfettered right to regulate content unless they enjoy monopoly status. If they enjoy a monopoly status, they may no longer claim a right to monopolize the regulation of content.

475. Professor C. Edwin Baker, for instance, discusses government intervention and ownership regulations to support a free press in "Press Rights and Government Power to Structure the Press," 34 Univ. of Miami Law Review 821.

476. Lawrence Tribe, Constitutional Choices (Cambridge, MA 1985).

477. Ibid., 193.

478. Ibid., 198.

479. U.S. Postal Serv. v. Council of Greenburgh Civic Assn., 453 U.S. 114 (1981); Citizens Against Rent Control v. City of Berkeley, 454 U.S. 290 (1981).

480. See Baker, "Press Rights," 819. Professor Baker discusses two kinds of rights: defensive rights and offensive rights. Access rights are categorized as offensive rights, whereas defensive rights protect press enterprises from government appropriation and interference. For instance, protection against searches and seizures are defensive rights. According to Professor Baker, "Offensive rights give the press enterprise or the reporters special rights of action or special rights to obtain materials outside the institutional boundaries of the press. The right to refuse to cooperate is defensive; the demand for cooperation is offensive." Generally speaking, defensive rights are rights against government intrusions.

481. For instance, in the revised marketplace theory of the free press clause, the Court may be required to give tax benefits to an entering newspaper by extending the holding in Minneapolis Star & Tribune v. Commissioner of Revenue, 103 S.Ct. 1365 (1983). In a previous case, the Court had outlined the touchstones of constitutionally acceptable government regulation of the press. First, the impartial distribution of information must not be affected. Second, the law must not constitute a special burden on the press. Curtis Publishing Co. v. Butts, 388 U.S. 130, 151 (1967). Indeed, the Minneapolis Star and Tribune case was decided on an analysis of the government's role toward the press and of the structure of the press in society. The case did not rely merely on the prior restraint doctrine. Indeed, the Court validated its attacks not only because it discriminated between newspapers but also because it differentiated between newspapers and other entities. Thus, the Court seems to recognize that the industrial framework of the press deserves special attention in that a structural diversity made up of independent competitive media outlets is necessary. See 103 S.Ct. at 1372. In Grosjean v. American Press Company, 297 U.S. 233, the Court held that the First Amendment barred a tax imposed so as to potentially discourage the widespread circulation of a newspaper. This holding again

illustrates the value and function of a free press--a structurally diverse industry made up of independent and competitive newspapers.

482. For instance, under the revised marketplace theory of the free press clause, the Court may be required to give tax benefits to an entering newspaper by extending the holding in <u>Minneapolis Star & Tribune v. Commissioner of Revenue</u>, 103 S. Ct. 1365 (1983). In a previous case, the Court had outlined the touchstones of constitutionally acceptable government regulation of the press. First, the impartial distribution of information must not be affected. Second, the law must not constitute a special burden on the press. <u>Curtis Publishing Co. v. Butts</u>, 388 U.S. 130, 151 (1967). Indeed, the <u>Minneapolis Star and Tribune</u> case was decided on an analysis of the government's role toward the press and of the structure of the press in society. The case did not rely merely on the prior restraint doctrine. Indeed, the Court invalidated the tax not only because it discriminated between newspapers but also because it differentiated between newspapers and other entities. Thus, the Court seems to recognize that the industrial framework of the press deserves special attention in that a structural diversity made up of independent competitive media outlets is necessary. <u>See</u> 103 S.Ct. at 1372. Likewise, in <u>Grosjean v. American Press Company</u>, 297 U.S. 233, the Court held that the First Amendment barred a tax imposed so as to potentially discourage the widespread circulation of a newspaper. This holding again illustrates the value and function of a free press--a structurally diverse industry made up of independent and competitive newspapers.

483. Barrow, "The Fairness Doctrine," 686.

484. For data relating to the concentration of ownership in the newspaper industry, see B. Rucker, <u>The First Freedom</u> (Carbondale: Southern Illinois Univ. Press, 1968). Also, see Schmidt, <u>Freedom of the Press</u>, 38-39, quoting from Baker and Ball, <u>Violence and the Media</u>, staff report to the National Commission on the Causes and Prevention of Violence:

> When the constitution was adopted . . . the individual could make his opinions known by . . . getting a printer to put up a broadside . . . . With relative ease he could have an impact . . . . A newspaper might have been started with relatively little capital by one whose views are strong enough to demand that they be aired . . . . the media today comprised institutions far different from the press of two centuries ago . . . . The ability of any single man to gain access to the marketplace of ideas has become all but extinct . . . .

485. Barrow, "The Fairness Doctrine", 686. Today, the capital required to publish a newspaper is so large that entry into that industry is very difficult and the owners tend to be on the wealthy end of the economic scale.

486. See <u>Branzburg v. Hayes</u>, 408 U.S. at 725-26 (Stewart, J., dissenting), and at 721 (Douglas, J., dissenting); <u>Houchins V. K. O. E. D., Inc.</u>, 438 U.S. at 30-34 (Stevens, J., dissenting).

487. Maister, "Journistic Silence and Governmental Speech, 323.

488. Ibid., 355.

489. Ibid., 355-56.

490. Ibid., 356.

491. The press plays a governmental role insofar as it is the arbiter and advocate of the public's interest in government. See <u>Branzburg v. Hayes</u>, 408 U.S. at 725 (Stewart, J., dissenting)

492. For a summary discussion of this equalizing function, see Maister, "Journalistic Silence in Governmental Speech," 372-76.

493. Barron, "Access to the Press," 1658. Professor Barron criticizes Justice Black's statement that newspapers be entirely immune from libel actions where public officials are being attached. <u>New York Times Company v. Sullivan</u>, 376 U.S. 254, 297 (1964) (Black, J., concurring).

494. Leonard, <u>Power of the Press</u>, 215.

495. Daniel C. Hallin, <u>The Uncensored War: The Media and Vietnam</u> (N.Y. 1986).

496. Daniel C. Hallin, "The Media, the War in Vietnam, and Political Support: A Critique of the These of an Oppositional Media," <u>Journal of Politics</u> 46 (February 1984) 2-24).

497. Thomas R. Dye, <u>What's Wrong With America</u>? (Englewood Cliffs, N.J. 1986) 125.

498. Ibid.

499. Barron, "Access to the Press," 1658. This is Professor Barron's criticism of the New York Times v. Sullivan decision.

500. Justice White's opinions include the following propositions: (1) reporters are not privileged in matters of offering testimony about criminal activity, Branzburg v. Hayes, 408 U.S. 665 (1972); (2) newsroom files are not privileged in criminal subpoena situations, Zercher v. Standford Daily, 436 U.S. 547 (1978); and (3) there exists no privilege regarding the editorial process of responsible parties when the published material is alleged to be false and damaging, Herbert v. Landow, 99 S. Ct. 1635 (1979). Furthermore, Justice White's dissent in Gertz v. Robert Welch, Inc. 500., 418 U.S. 323, 399 (1974), states that "The First Amendment was intended to guarantee free expression, not to create a privileged industry."

501. 418 U.S. at 390, 391, 400.

502. In Branzburg, White writes that the advocacy of liberalized freedoms for the press may become misguided. 408 U.S. at 692-93. According to White, the aim is not to form a privileged industry, 418 U.S. at 392. In fact, "The First Amendment does not invalidate every incidental burdening of the press that may result from the enforcement of civil or criminal statutes of general applicability." 408 U.S. at 682.

503. The protections already given to the press can be summed up as follows: New York Times gave a grant of extraordinary protection from libel suits, 403 U.S. at 730; Miami Herald invalidated the right-of-reply statute and held that the government could not inject itself into the editorial process, 418 U.S. at 259; Gertz refused to reject the essentiality of a free press, 418 U.S. at 398; and Zurcher gave a standard of scrupulous exactitude when materials protected by the First Amendment are subject to search and seizure, 436 U.S. at 566.

504. Failure of the news media to cover America's "news cartel" was the most under-reported story of 1987, according to Project Censored.

505. See Barron, "Access to the Press," 1641 ("But if ever there were a self-operating marketplace of ideas, it has long ceased to exist").

506. Ibid. , 1643.

507. This is because the marketplace of ideas concept has "rested on the assumption that protecting the right of expression is equivalent to providing for it." Ibid.,1647-48.

508. Ibid., 1648.

509. See chapter on media concentration in Schmidt, Freedom of the Press, 43.

510. Schmidt perceives a danger lurking beneath the marketplace of ideas concept. This concept developed as a shield against government regulation of speech, but it can also be used--as the access movement proves--as a sword for government intrusion. Its risks arise from its seemingly exclusive emphasis on the value of efficiency. The danger is that thinking about First Amendment problems in that way alone may lead us to shortchange ourselves by forgetting what is essential to our integrity as a people. Bollinger, review of Freedom of the Press, 1361.

In answering this criticism, the revised marketplace model does not rely totally on efficiency or on trying to maximize the amount of speech in society.

511. Bezanson, "New Free Press Guarantee, " 759.

512. When the framers drafted the First Amendment, a true marketplace of ideas existed in which there was relatively easy access to the channels of communication. Miami Herald Publishing Company v. Tornillo, 418 U.S. 248.

513. Ibid., 250. Professor Schmidt has also outlined the concentration in the communications industry in Freedom of the Press, 39-45.

514. Owen, Economics and Freedom of Expression, 26-28, 186-87.